Real Presence

Real Presence

The Sacramentality of the Present Moment

Michael Hickey

HAMILTON BOOKS

HAMILTON BOOKS

Bloomsbury Publishing Inc, 1385 Broadway, New York, NY 10018, USA
Bloomsbury Publishing Plc, 50 Bedford Square, London, WC1B 3DP, UK
Bloomsbury Publishing Ireland, 29 Earlsfort Terrace, Dublin 2, D02 AY28, Ireland

BLOOMSBURY and the Diana logo are trademarks of Bloomsbury Publishing Plc

First published in the United States of America 2025

Cover image © Pascal Deloche/Stone/Getty Images
Created by Michael Hickey

Bloomsbury Publishing Inc does not have any control over, or responsibility for, any third-
party websites referred to or in this book. All internet addresses given in this book were
correct at the time of going to press. The author and publisher regret any inconvenience
caused if addresses have changed or sites have ceased to exist, but can accept no
responsibility for any such changes.

A catalog record for this book is available from the Library of Congress.

ISBN: PB: 978-0-76188-071-4
ePDF: 978-0-76188-073-8
eBook: 978-0-76188-072-1

Typeset by Deanta Global Publishing Services, Chennai, India

For product safety related questions contact productsafety@bloomsbury.com.

To find out more about our authors and books visit www.bloomsbury.com
and sign up for our newsletters.

Generally, by the time you are Real, most of your hair has been loved off, and your eyes drop out and you get loose in the joints and very shabby. But these things don't matter at all, because once you are Real you can't be ugly, except to people who don't understand.

—*The Velveteen Rabbit*, a Children's Story by Margery Williams

Contents

Reality

What Is Reality?

Reality is the quality or state of being real, authentic, and genuine. It has a basis in actual fact and truth. It includes everything that is, no matter whether observable or comprehensible, visible or invisible. When something is real, it is said to be authentic. Its origin is genuine and supported by evidence. The word "authentic" itself has the same root as "author," which means creator or originator. Both of these words have the same root in the Greek, which is *autos*, and it translates to our English word, "self." When something is real, it is also considered as genuine. This word comes into our language from the Latin word *genuinus*, which means "natural." The root of this word is the same in both the Latin and the English languages, and it is *genus*, which defines someone or something of a certain kind of real species. Reality is far more complex than what our immediate sense experience can tell us. The senses of seeing, hearing, tasting, touching, and smelling provide us with our immediate sense experience, but reality and the criteria for what we consider "real" in our world are mediated by meaning. Only the Holy Spirit can show us the right way to approach what all of us call "reality."

The real is known to us through judgments and beliefs which give us meaning, and our personal sense experiences of reality alone are simply not enough to tell us what is real. We also need other people to be involved in order to gain our own understanding of reality. Having other people relate to us what reality is to them can be helpful to begin to form our own understanding of it.

First, because appearances can be deceiving, there is no guarantee that what we are personally seeing, perceiving, or immediately experiencing through our senses is what is real. Intuition or a kind of sixth sense beyond our five senses can be helpful here, but is not completely adequate to convey the fuller meaning of what is real. Because reality is dynamic and mediated by meaning, what occurs is that reality constantly changes as meaning changes over time.

Words can also die a static death in time, so reality, because it is dynamic, must necessarily transcend the words alone. Take the word "family" for example. On the one hand, we are all convinced that a family is a reality and that it exists. We speak about families, we think about families, and we see them as a reality. Each of us usually thinks of ourselves as being part of some known family. Yet, none of us can really "touch" a family or "see" a family. A family is more than what we can see or touch on the physical level through our sensory experience. What a family "is" in reality is a judgment and belief, and is a reality that is constituted with meaning for us.

Because it is "mediated by meaning," the meaning can shift over time. For example, there used to exist only the nuclear family or traditional family consisting of a mother, a father, and some children. Today, in many minds, there exists the extended family, single-parent family, communal family, church family, partnered family, work family, and so on. Because the family as a reality is constituted with meaning, for many of us, the reality has changed as the meaning has changed over time. Reality can then only be dynamically understood over time through judgments and beliefs held in common.

In discussing reality, I should state at the outset that what I will be focusing on in this book will be "reality of being." This is different from what we might call restricted categories of reality, such as mathematics or hypothetical and logical categories, which can be affirmed rationally or quantitatively. Reality of being is affirmed by the living of life, experiential wisdom, spiritual experience, and individual or collective consciousness, which can often arise only after prayerful reflection and contemplation of mystery. It can lead one further into prayerful silence, universal wonder, and the increasing love of God and others.

In the dynamic state of love of God, our consciousness is different from our knowledge. To quote Catholic theologian Bernard Lonergan:

Consciousness is just experience. Knowledge is a compound of experience, understanding, and judging. Because the dynamic state is conscious without being known, it is an experience of mystery.

Therefore, reality of being can be a conscious experience, though not fully realized or known. Because reality is dynamic, constituted with meaning, and the meaning itself can be continually changing over time, reality must have a future dimension with an unknown and unrealized quality. In that reality has this future dimension, and the future is unknown and unrealized, especially for us as human beings, we can only conclude that in many cases, mystery is the true home of reality.

Reality of Being

Unlike mathematics, reality of being cannot be confined to a restricted category of reality because it is not univocal. It cannot have only one meaning for all because each of us is a different being with a different reality of being, even though we are universally and collectively called human beings. Our personal experiences, interactions, observations, perceptions, formation, and development have shaped our individual reality. In this instance, reality is experienced by only one individual. This reality might be similar and held in common with others but at times might be simply unique to oneself and one's own being. Much of what we deem as "spiritual" occurs in this dimension of reality. Therefore, when we refer to reality of being, we are not referring to one individual or specific reality but to many.

Ontology is the philosophical study of the nature of reality of being in general, as well as some of the basic categories of being such as "existence" and "essence." The study makes inquiries into being in as much as it is being or is being-in-reality. It tries to answer the question initially posed by Aristotle, "What does it mean to be?" Ontology is part of a broader branch of the study of philosophy heavily influenced by Aristotle called Metaphysics. The philosophical study of Ontology today seems to be equivalent to a study about existence in relation to reality of being, with little or no emphasis on essence.

In many ways, this seems to have led to a very static definition of reality. This is not something that developed out of Aristotle's Metaphysics, as he saw a world of difference between existence and essence and saw the value of both in relation to reality of being.

Today, for example, the *Oxford English Dictionary* (as does most English dictionaries) defines "reality" in the following terms with a strong bias in the direction of rendering its meaning strictly on the level of "existence" with little regard for "essence." Its definition of "reality" is as follows:

1. The state of things as they actually exist, as opposed to an idealistic or notational idea of them.
2. A thing that is actually experienced or seen.
3. The quality of being lifelike.
4. The state or quality of having existence or substance.

Today's dictionary definitions seem to have led to a very static and not a dynamic definition of reality. It renders an understanding of reality to be something synonymous with existence. They do not seem to consider spirituality, and they make little or no connection between existence and essence.[1]

Essence and Existence in Reality

In any discussion of reality, one must consider "being" not only in terms of "isness" but also in terms of "becoming." We get our English word "essence" from the Greek word, *ousia* (being), and later from the Latin word, *esse* (to be) or (is). Essence can be translated to mean: "The act of being or the very nature of something as opposed to its existence."

It is primarily from the ancient philosopher Aristotle that we get our modern thoughts about essence. Aristotle was a student of Plato. To Plato, to see the "real world" was to see the "ideal world" and to see it as a system of essences. In many ways, to Plato, the idea or ideal was "the real." What Plato called idea or ideal, Aristotle called essence, and its opposite he referred to as matter. He saw matter as just "stuff"—pure potential with no actuality. Essence is what provides the shape or form, or purpose to matter. Essence has no substance or solidity. Therefore, essence and matter need each other.

In the early Christian community, the Gospel writer John would tell us more about the reality of being, essence, and existence in the opening words of his Gospel of Jesus Christ, written around 90 AD:

> In the beginning was the Word, and the Word was with God, and the Word was God. He was in the beginning with God. All things came to be through him, and without him nothing came to be. (Jn 1:1–3)

Later, Christian, Jewish, and Islamic medieval philosophers made Aristotle's writings the groundwork of their commentaries as they expanded and enriched his philosophical thinking in the light of revelation. Among the more notable of these were Averroes, Moses Maimonides, Francisco Suarez, and Thomas Aquinas. It was Aquinas who took the thoughts of all of these men, as well as others before him, to synchronize Aristotle's philosophy with Christian revelation. His masterpiece, the *Summa Theologica*, would have much to tell us concerning the reality of being, essence, and existence:

> "One" does not add any reality to "being," but is only a negation of division; for "one" means undivided "being." This is the very reason why "one" is the same as "being." Now every being is either simple or compound, but what is simple is undivided, both actually and potentially. What is compound has not being while its parts are divided, but after they make up and compose it. Hence it is manifest that the being of anything consists in undivision; and hence it is that everything guards its unity as it guards its being.

Aquinas maintained that essence and existence are in God and that all of the created order participates in the reality of being of God. He would write, "Everything exists because it has being." But he further maintained in his *Summa* that only in God were essence and existence the same (e.g., God is good; God is love). If one's essence in the created order is not their being, they still participate by existing in the reality of being itself. Therefore, every created reality participates in the reality of the being of God, the Creator, whose essence and existence are the same.

Many modern theologians today have followed and built on the writings of St. Thomas Aquinas by continuing in the Thomistic Tradition. One of the most prominent theologians of our time, the late Fr. Karl Rahner, S. J., who has himself been called a "Transcendental Thomist," has written over 4,000 books, essays, and theological encyclopedias on Catholic/Christian theology and philosophic thought. A good summation of his theology can be found by looking at his four-volume theological encyclopedia called *Sacramentum Mundi,* combined with his three-inch-thick theological handbook titled *Foundations of Christian Faith.* Here, Fr. Rahner very often discusses reality of being in terms of what he refers to as a "Supernatural Existential." He does so, first as an ontological statement, then as an appeal to reality, and then finally as a realization of grace in a radical way. Fr. Rahner envisions the "Supernatural Existential" to be a "permanent modification of the human spirit which transforms its natural dynamism into an ontological drive to the God of grace and glory." He concludes that it is essence which realizes ("makes real") matter; it is essence which spiritualizes matter. In other words, any ontological discussion concerning reality of being is not complete unless at some point it comes around to discussing either essence or spirituality and not simply existence. Both what is actual and what is potential must be considered in determining what is "real" in the context of "being." If reality of being restricts itself to a static discussion only at the level of human existence as we know it, it will always be rational and incomplete knowledge at best. In the worst sense, it will never become a meaningful dialogue about either consciousness or reality.

Because "reality of being" must always take into account the potential act of "becoming," within any human being, its orientation is necessarily toward the future, which for any human person is always shrouded in mystery. Only in God, who is both a Transcendent Reality and the Holy Mystery, can we begin to realize our true reality of being, for it is only in God that we live and move and have our being. When a human being asks themselves or someone asks us, "Who are you?" this is primarily a questioning of our reality. Self-centered pride sets us apart from others, from God, and finally from our true self, which can only be realized in God, whose essence and existence are both exactly the same. In both Christianity and Judaism, God is considered the "Absolute Reality," being the foundation of everything that is and the end toward which everyone and everything points. God is the "Alpha and Omega," the beginning and the end of everything. Renowned theologian Teilhard de

Chardin, S. J., has often called this endpoint "The Omega Point." The Omega Point will coincide with the Second Coming of Christ (The Parousia) when the Universal Christ will overcome all sickness, hunger, suffering, and even death. He will lift the veil that separates mystery and reality and create for us a new heaven and a new earth, as all that is our existing reality will essentially be transformed.

Reality and Truth

Truth is a judgment, proposition, or idea that is true because it is in accord with reality and is free from error, distortion, lies, and misrepresentation. The more we arrive at the discovery of truth in our world, the clearer is our understanding of reality; the less truth, the greater is the illusion of reality. There is no single definition of truth upon which most people can agree. Various theories of truth are hotly debated such as what constitutes truth, how to define or identify it, and whether truth is subjective, relative, objective, or absolute.

In the Christian New Testament, Jesus tells us that the word He brings is truth—that He Himself is the way, the truth, and the life—the Holy Spirit will be the Spirit of truth, which will lead us to all truth, and the truth will set us free. To define the truth is one thing; to know that we have judged truly is quite another. To actually be able to define truth involves judgment and belief to distinguish truth from error and reality from illusion. We cannot define that which we cannot distinguish, but it is often with our perception of reality and the appearance of things that is the basis on which our judgments are made and may not necessarily be their essential nature.

Therefore, in discerning truth, we should not allow irrelevant considerations to affect our perception of reality. We should also avoid any rush to judgment as much as possible, and make every attempt to rid ourselves of bias, prejudice, and an over-anxious will to believe something is true before we discern that it is. Thomas Aquinas believed that truth could be defined as:

That which was in conformity with truth in the divine mind of God.

Theoretically, since whatever is true should be good and just, true judgments ought to result in good consequences and produce just and loving outcomes. When this is applied to ourselves, we know that although it is virtuous to speak what we believe to be the truth, to be in conformity with the divine mind of God, we should always attempt to speak the truth in love so that we will also be in accord with reality. Love is God's truth because God is love and love is God's reality. Once again, this is true because God is the only Being whose essence and existence are really the same.

Reality and Belief

If faith can be seen as personal knowledge of God, then belief is the formulation of the body of knowledge of God through communal faith. It can also be seen as an acceptance of truth without clear and convincing evidence or concrete proof which we verify personally. Belief can help us to articulate the knowledge we have of God. In a progression, faith leads to theology (faith seeking understanding), and then theology leads to belief. These should not be seen as static concepts as they are dynamic and continuously impact each other and interrelate because they can change.

Faith, theology, and belief should always be in accord with the truth, and the truth should always be in accord with reality. Both Augustine and Aquinas, after him, maintained

I believe therefore I understand.

The truths of faith will always provide some degree of understanding and make sense to one who is a believer. To an unbeliever, they will be utter nonsense, because for those who believe, no proof is necessary; for those who do not believe, no proof will ever be enough. Belief, then, can never prove the existence of God as a truth that is in accord with reality. Through the inward movement and acceptance of grace, it can only try to ground that belief in an understanding of the reality, which can only be experienced as transcendent while remaining at the same time a Holy Mystery.

Both truth and belief will often involve others in reality. Although truth is always in accord with reality, the fact of the matter is that there are far more truths that we simply are led to believe than we can possibly verify personally or critically by assessing all of the data on which scientific proofs are based. We also live in a modern world where the flow of information is massive, and the data we receive inundates us. A tsunami occurs in Indonesia, an earthquake disrupts all life in Haiti, a plane crash happens in Pakistan, or a volcano erupts in Iceland; we receive information like this almost daily. We have no way to verify it as truth in reality on a personal or individual level. We, as human beings who seek the truth, must often do so by believing others who share reality with us. We have no choice in many instances but to trust the truth to others without personally verifying or proving its accuracy and evidence. Without our own personal verification, the question then becomes for any of us . . . "What truths are we to believe are in accord with reality?"

Therefore, if most of what we accept as reality every day can never be individually and personally verified, then in the final analysis, faith, belief, and truth can only be inner realities. Although inner realities are personal realities, they are not necessarily private realities. They are realities held communally. The further question becomes "who and what are we believing in our acceptance of reality both personally and communally?" In the final analysis, we are all believers; we have no other choice. For example, the Bible is a record of faith, belief, truth, and reality as seen by others before us spanning thousands of years. Christians are asked to believe that this book is not simply a human construct but also the self-communication of God—a living presence and Transcendent Reality who inspired the human writers. It carries an authority as an inspired and recorded report of faith, belief, truth, and reality that is unequaled.

So, trusting the truth as examined, personally witnessed, believed, and then communicated by Matthew, Mark, Luke, John, Paul, and a biblical host of others before us is preferential for many of us who are attempting to understand our reality and stand in awe of God's reality. On the other hand, it is certainly no different than the way much of the world entrusts their truth to countless unknown others every day without their personal and individual verification. This is being done to assess what each of us simply and commonly refers to each day as "reality."

To quote renowned theologian Teilhard de Chardin, S. J.:

> At the present time many believers, to avoid the anxieties that contact with reality might renew in them, allow a veil of conventional answers to cover the mysteries of life. . . . We are not human beings having a spiritual experience, we are spiritual beings having a human experience.

Love, the Ultimate Reality

The human person has a dynamism within which orients them toward an Absolute Being who is a Transcendent Reality. Love is a keyword for this mysterious dynamism in which the true and whole man is drawn away from his or her own reality and into the incomprehensible mystery we call "God." Christ's love is divine love (*agape*, Gk.). It is God's love shared with humanity, and it is unconditional, infinite, self-giving, and has the welfare of others at its heart. Only Jesus Christ has fully and perfectly "realized" this love on earth, but it is His mark in anyone who is "self-realizing" through the Holy Spirit.

Love is the essence of being real, and it is the ultimate reality of being. Because it is a spiritual reality, it is dynamic (*dynamis,* Gk.), and because it is dynamic, it is constantly in movement and can only be realized when we love and are being loved. Love must be spiritually experienced; otherwise, it cannot be known. Therefore, to quote theologian Karl Rahner, S. J., as well as others mentioned earlier:

> Love has primacy to any knowledge.

Through the acceptance of grace within, loving another begins with loving ourselves. It is impossible to love another person without holistically loving ourselves. This is implied in both Old Testament law and in Christ's words in all three New Testament synoptic Gospels concerning loving our neighbor as our "self" (Lev. 19:18; Mt. 19:19; Mk 12:31; Lk. 10:27). The Apostle Paul also confirms this in his letters (Rom. 13:9, Gal. 5:14) and Thomas Aquinas later takes this up in his *Summa* (Sum. Q. 25), not only referencing those prior scriptures but also the philosopher Aristotle (*Ethics* IX: 4,8). It is in coming to greater self-realization that we grow in the understanding of the meaning and importance of the word, "self," in the love dynamic.

As the ultimate spiritual reality, love alone has the potential to unite human beings in such a way as to complete them and bring them to perfection, but because God is the only Being where essence and existence are the same, it is perfectly realized love as "God is love." Therefore, if our essence and existence as human beings are not perfectly realized love as is the case with God, then it can only be "change" as we orient ourselves to this perfectly loving God by loving others and being loved. The more we become "lovers," the more love becomes "realized" in our lives and the lives of others.

Love loses its energy and spiritual power if it remains anonymous. All love is self-surrender, as we cannot really love without loving another person and losing ourselves in that person. That makes love the most personal of all realities. Because it is the most personal reality, it becomes the most universal and ultimate reality for each of us and has a dynamism and a dimension that is universal. This is not to say that we personally have enough loving potential for all humanity, but only that loving the one or loving the few has both personal and universal consequences. When the universe assumes a face, heart, and personality for us, then it becomes a most personal and universal ultimate reality.

Love's source is the self-communication of the Spirit of God. If we have had the experience of loving others and being loved, that would indicate that love must have a real source. If love has a real source, where does it really end? If our own birth was not the source of love, then how can our own death be the end? Believing that love is the ultimate reality would negate the belief that death would be our final reality; it would have to transcend the reality of death. Because love is dynamic, expansive, and never ends (1 Cor 13:13), our own death cannot lead to un-love, un-being, or un-reality. It can only lead us back to the source of love, which is present in God, the Holy Mystery and Transcendent Reality. The goal of love is union with whom we love and want to be near; that is why God's love is the greatest spiritual power and ultimate reality. It must have endurance, permanence, and last not only beyond death, space, and time but throughout eternity. After our last breath in this world, our faith, which is now in an unseen reality, will become seen, and our hope will become wisdom (realized experience) as it moves from an unrealized future into a present "realized reality." We will then be united in love as both our essence and existence because:

> God is love, and whoever abides in love abides in God, and God abides in them. (Jn 4:16)

There is no separation in the Trinity. Therefore, when faith moves to sight and hope yields from "becoming" to our self-realization as fully "being" in God, there will, in the end, be only perfect love as we become fully realized into being in God and thus united in love, the ultimate reality, as One with the Father, Son, and Holy Spirit.[2,3,4,5,6]

Notes

As per the endnote citations at the conclusion of this first chapter, the following are the key theological source materials that were utilized as reference for the writing of this book. Many of these endnote references in Chapter 1 will be cited as endnote reference source materials in the remaining chapters of this book. Furthermore, all the many biblical references utilized throughout the remainder of this book will be taken from the version of the New American Bible cited below in footnote #6. They will be referenced only one time here below with this footnote.

1   "Reality," Merriam-Webster Dictionary, online dictionary, https://www.merriam
   -webster.com/dictionary/reality; see also EncyclopediaBritannica, online https://
   www.britannica.com/dictionary/reality#:~:text=Britannica%20Dictionary
   %20definition%20of%20REALITY,%5B%3Dthe%20truth%5D; see also Oxford
   English Dictionary (London: Oxford University, 2008), https://www.oed.com/
   dictionary/reality_n?tl=true
2   Richard McBrien, ed., *Catholicism* (New York: HarperCollins, 1994), pp. 1248–9.
3   "Reality," Karl Rahner, ed., *Encyclopedia of Theology, The Concise Sacramentum
   Mundi* (New York: Seabury Press, 1973, pp. 1324–6); *Foundations of Christian
   Faith* (New York: Seabury Press, 1978).
4   Pierre Teilhard de Chardin, quotes online, https://www.brainyquote.com/lists/
   authors/top-10-pierre-teilhard-de-chardi-quotes?gad_source=1&gclid=Cj0KCQi

A4fi7BhC5ARIsAEV1Yib9W5poZeQeL_6KAUW1o8FIAXpOrSXFrnWto3eFD vyMzFD3yRDHfwsaAmq8EALw_wcB, see also Pierre Teilhard de Chardin, *Phenomenon of Man* (New York: Harper & Row, 1975).

5 Kevin Knight, ed., *Catholic Encyclopedia*, online version New Advent; L. Walker, "Truth/ Reality." *The Catholic Encyclopedia* (New York: Robert Appleton Company, 2012). http://www.newadvent.org/cathen/15073a.htm; T. Aquinas, complete *Summa Theologica*, online, New Advent, https://www.newadvent.org/summa/

6 *New American Bible*, St. Joseph Edition, UCCB approved, online (New York: Catholic Book Publishing Co., 1980), also online-http:// bible UCCB.org/bible .htm

2

Presence

The late Fr. Henri Nouwen has been quoted as saying:

> The real enemies of our life are the "oughts" and the "ifs." They pull us backward into the unalterable past and forward into the unpredictable future. But real life takes place in the present moment.[1]

Reality is based on universal truths, both seen and unseen; presence is based on the now-moment in time and space as a reflection of eternity.

What Is Presence?

A human being's presence most often implies that they are physically here and show up in person. For one to have presence may also infer that they project poise, carriage, distinguished bearing, or possess a certain air of authority. To be present further implies that one is focused on the current moment in the here and now and undistracted by the future or the past. However, the presence in a person or being that you cannot see, but you are somehow aware of, often implies a presence of a spiritual or mystical nature.

When we hear the word "presence" we think of a relationship between two or more people. We are present to someone when we are aware of them and vice versa. Presence implies reality of being because, for example, we are not exactly or fully present to a stone, nor is a stone exactly present to us. Presence can also transcend the dimensions of time and space. The eminent biblical theologian, the late Fr. Dan Harrington S. J., may be present to me even though he has passed away and is not physically present where I am. As my former faculty adviser at Weston/Boston College School of Theology and Ministry, he is present to me mentally, intellectually, and spiritually. Much about what he taught me concerning the Living Word of God can be brought alive again and again in my mind and heart. Another example—I may be in one location and my wife, Terri, in another, but as soon as I bring her to mind, I think about her lovingly, and bring her into my heart, then she becomes present to me. So, presence may imply physical or bodily reality and nearness, but not in every instance. If there is spiritual intimacy of mind or loving hearts and souls, presence can be seen to transcend time and space.

To say that God has immanent presence is to say that He is present in time and space and that He is near to us. It is because God loves us that He wants to be near to us. There is no biblical term that captures all of what theologians might have to say about God's transcendent presence, as it is something that involves eternity and is far more an experience of a spiritual nature. The idea of immanence is helpfully summarized in the Bible with the term "*Emmanuel*, God with us" (Isa. 7:14; 8:8; Mt. 1:23).[2]

The Incarnation of Jesus Christ is a supreme example of God's immanent presence among us. Jesus became one of us in the Incarnation. He became man, took upon Himself the likeness of men; He lived and died among us. Born as a child in Bethlehem, Jesus was no distant God come from far away or unconcerned about the plight of us mere mortals. As St. Athanasius so aptly put it: "Jesus actually became what we are so that we might become like he is."[3]

From a Christian perspective, to be present to the Lord implies that we are prayerfully oriented to God through the Holy Spirit of Jesus Christ as an inner reality and properly grounded in a Christian community of worship where God can become really present to us in Word and Sacrament.

Old and New Testament Presence

Beginning with the earliest accounts of Israel's recorded biblical history, it is Yahweh's (I Am Who Am) presence among His people that distinguishes Israel from all other surrounding nations. Although God had indicated His hidden and mysterious presence to the nation of Israel on many prior occasions (e.g., the rainbow signifying His covenant), Yahweh, as God Almighty, is first revealed and made present to Moses in the burning bush. The Ark of the Covenant would soon become the intended locus of Yahweh's divine presence (Exod. 25:22).

The rabbis of Israel, not wanting to use God's personal name, would begin using the name *Shekinah* (Glorious Presence) as a surrogate for the name Yahweh (Exod. 19:16–18; 40: 34–38), as well as the common names for a deity such as *El Shaddai* or *Elohim* (God Almighty) to represent the divine presence. Because God Almighty, as king of Israel, was present in the Ark of the Covenant and stood at the head of Israel's armies, they should fear no enemy. The Ark of the Covenant was placed in a tent until Solomon later built a temple and placed it in the Holy of Holies. The divine presence often took the form of a cloud that filled the tent.

The temple played an important part in the life of Israel's people as it was considered the house where God would dwell and be present among His people. When the Ark was captured, the Israelites became very much alarmed and interpreted it as a sign that God Almighty was no longer present among His people. There was much dancing and rejoicing when the Ark was returned, and King David brought it to Jerusalem, where it was kept.

Gradually, in the history of Israel, the people would come to understand that God Almighty could not be limited to only being present in their temple. They believed that Yahweh was in their midst (*Emmanuel*, God with us) and near to them, but as God Almighty, He was transcendent as well and dwelled in the highest heavens above the clouds. Later in Israel's history, many of the prophets began to envision that a messiah-king in the line of King David would one day be born. He would be present in their midst to lead his people into the eternal Kingdom of God. More than 700 years before the birth of Jesus of Nazareth, Hosea, the prophet of Israel, would foretell this:

> He will bind our wounds—He will revive us after two days, on the third day,
> he will raise us up to live in his presence. (Hos. 6: 2–3)

Jesus of Nazareth, born in a stable in Bethlehem to a humble virgin, was not who the Jews were expecting to come into the world as their king. The evangelist John, in his Gospel, tells us:

> In the beginning was the Word, and the Word was with God, and the Word
> was God. . . . And the Word became flesh and made his dwelling among us,

and we saw his glory, the glory as of the Father's only Son, full of grace and truth. (Jn 1:1, 14)

His own people did not recognize Jesus as the *Shekinah*, (Glorious Presence). His own followers could not even understand how or why a messiah-king would have to suffer the passion of the cross or what "rising from the dead" could possibly mean.

Following Jesus' resurrection and ascension, He is now present at the right hand of the Father in heaven. The Holy Spirit sent by Jesus Christ from the Father, is the manifestation of His presence among us as believers within the Body of Christ. It is our hope of the future glory that was promised. His inner presence within the community of believers through the power of the Holy Spirit is now our guarantee that He will keep His promise and be with us always until the end of the world. Jesus Christ became for us the new tabernacle of God's presence and the *Shekinah*, (Glorious Presence). Finally, Christ's real presence among us, particularly in the celebration of the Eucharistic Banquet (see Chapters 11 and 12 of this book), is what continues to actively commemorate His presence by being *Emmanuel*-God with us.[4]

Omnipresence

The prefix, *omni*, in Latin means "all," so to say that God is omnipresent is to say that God is present everywhere and at all times. It implies that God is present throughout the universe and beyond the boundaries of space and time. Although God is present in all time and space, God is not locally limited to any time or space. God is everywhere and in every now-moment on into eternity. God's omnipresence carries with it the understanding that the Lord is also Omnipotent, which means that God is all-powerful and in total control of Himself and His creation. God also possesses Omniscience, which means that He is all-knowing and the ultimate criterion of truth and falsity and the source of absolute truth and reality. He is the source of love and knowledge. Together, these define God's Lordship and presence and yield a rich theological understanding of creation, grace, providence, power, authority, and salvation.

No molecule or atom is so small that God is not fully present to it, nor is any galaxy so enormous that God does not circumscribe it with His providence and unconditional love. As the Holy Mystery, God is the primal cause and ground of all reality, whose center is everywhere and whose circumference is nowhere. In that God is the Holy Mystery, He is transcendentally present to all of His creation, while at the same time remaining in close relationship to all of His created reality. First and foremost, God is present in the person of His Son, the Lord Jesus Christ (Col. 2:19), whose Holy Spirit is also present to us sacramentally within the Body of Christ and throughout creation.

Finally, isn't it amazing that the Lord God, while yet remaining omnipresent to the entire universe and all creation, chose to limit Himself to become one of us as a tiny baby in a physical human body whose entire known universe was the womb of a virgin? The only erroneous limitations to God's omnipresence exist in the mistaken infinite projections of the finite human mind.[5]

Sacramental Presence: The Principle of Sacramentality

The Latin word *sacramentum* is a translation of the Greek word *mysterion*, and both can be translated into our English word "mystery." When the language of the early Christian church changed from Greek to Latin, the Greek word *mysterion* was occasionally translated by the Latin word *sacramentum*, and it is in this word that we find the biblical roots of the word "sacrament."

For the first eleven centuries of Christian history, the word "sacrament" was used in its more general sense, referring to the mysterious presence of God. Gradually, specific aspects of God's presence and plan for God's people began to be singled out and were incorporated into church rites such as Baptism, Matrimony, and Holy Orders, and called "Sacraments." However, this was not the early usage of the term. Taking the word "sacrament" in its broadest sense as a grace-filled sign of something sacred and hidden, we could say that the whole world is a vast sacramental system, in that material things are unto men the signs of things spiritual and sacred. What is sacramental can also be highly significant in pointing to the hidden presence of God in our midst. To quote Thomas Aquinas:

"Grace presupposes nature," or "Grace follows nature."

Grace is not an add-on. Therefore, a sacrament can be defined simply as "a visible sign of an invisible reality" or a "visible sign in reality of God's grace-filled presence as Holy Mystery." This would make the principle of sacramentality have its foundation in both mystery as well as reality. Both reality and mystery are merely words in the first place, but even the words themselves become sacramental in that they signify meaning to us and are more than a group of mere alphabetized letters.

God's presence can be revealed to us in images, words, events, and other visible realities, but will always remain more than that. If not, it is not God but merely an idol. All reality is imbued with the hidden presence of God. Therefore, all reality can be a visible sign of the presence of God—an external sign of something sacred, an outward sign of inward grace, and a natural signal of transcendence.

One might not be able to see the invisible in the visible per se, but we can have an experience of the divine in the human, the Creator in creation, grace in nature, the spiritual in the material, eternity in history or time, the supernatural in the natural, or the sacred in the ordinary. If all reality is being imbued with the hidden presence of God, this would necessarily imply to us that God can choose to become present to us and reveal Godself to us through other people, events, objects, the world and universe around us or for that matter anything tangible, visible, or happening in history. Because all reality can be symbolic and have a hidden character, God can reveal His presence to us through virtually everyone and everything around us. St. Francis of Assisi is a good example of someone who experienced this. He saw God mysteriously present in not only other people but also in the sun, moon, stars, and animals. Our God is a God of real presence—of mystery and majesty—is in everyone—is everywhere and anywhere. That should imply that all visible reality can be mediated to us by the unveiling of its meaning. Only God can lift the veil.

The greatest sacramental reality of the mysterious presence of God is Jesus Christ. Jesus is the ultimate sign and primal Sacrament of God's presence to us, through us, and in us in the presence and power of the Holy Spirit. It will be our response to the sacramental encounter of the presence of God in the

Holy Spirit of Jesus Christ throughout our lives that will determine our final destiny.[6]

In the 1700s, a French Jesuit, Fr. Jean Pierre De Caussade, coined the term "The Sacrament of the Present Moment." In his writings, he speaks about our abandonment to Divine Providence as we embrace the present now-moment and abandon ourselves to the Lord completely as a path to holiness. In doing this, we begin to experience each moment as a sacrament. We can choose right now to reject self-love and all forms of pride. Instead, we can choose, like a trusting child, to live for the Lord and love Him with all our heart, soul, mind, and strength, and follow His leading of the Holy Spirit from moment to moment. The past is gone, and the future hasn't arrived yet; all we have is this moment to live for the Lord and follow the leading of His Holy Spirit. Fr. De Caussade tells us:

> If we abandon ourselves to God, then the only rule for us is the duty of the present moment.[7]

It is a moment of grace, filled with surrender to God and abandonment to Divine Providence. It is this now-moment which is occurring both in time and as a reflection of the timelessness of eternity. I believe this is, in part, what Fr. De Caussade was trying to tell us about the importance of the present moment. It is a sacramental moment for me as I now write these words and for you as you read these words at a sacramental moment in time, and you pause to reflect on them.

Transcendental Presence

Our God, at one and the same time, is both a Transcendental Reality and Holy Mystery. Transcendental presence pertains to that dimension of the divine which is above and beyond the ordinary, seen, concrete, and tangible. Here, we might call this presence extraordinary or sacred. As a transcendental presence, God is totally other and is fully and completely present (omnipresent) to all life and reality. God's transcendental presence renders all created life and reality to be open to become someone or something more than it is already. It is our orientation to this transcendental presence in the depths of our inner being that can modify us as a human person and transform us through the divine offer and acceptance of grace. Ultimately, it is grace as the self-communication of God which we should consider as the abiding transcendental presence of God within our inner being. The transcendental presence of the Holy Spirit within by loving us can then transform and empower us to self-transcend and orient ourselves to God, Father, Son, and Holy Spirit, who is the primal cause and the presence of uncreated grace and love. The goal of love is union, and as was stated earlier, "God is love."

There is no point in our humanity whereby we can detach ourselves objectively and view God in the fullness of this transcendental presence because God is both always present within us in a personal and covenantal way while at the same time transcends above and beyond us as "other." God's transcendental presence allows us not only to see as far as the horizon before us but also to be filled with the faith and hope that beyond the horizon we can see, there exists another horizon that opens up. Transcendental presence in the human person can be found when we view our humanity not just as a collection of biological cells, behavioral responses, and the satisfaction of purely physical, social, cultural, and psychological needs or desires. We are transcendental beings inasmuch as we are oriented to the transcendental presence of God and accept God's offer of grace through the presence of the Holy Spirit within. God's full transcendental presence not only escapes the bounds of our logic and experience but, because God is wholly other/Holy Other, we can also come to know that this transcendental presence we call "God" is within, above, and beyond us, as well as all around us through faith and our experience of being loved and loving others. Jesus tells us that "the Kingdom of God is in your midst." This implies that it is not something totally in the future. It is coming to be in the ongoing history of the world—in this present moment in active love. As we discussed, it is for us, "the sacrament of the present moment." If we believe that the Kingdom of God is in Jesus Christ and that He is in our midst, then we live presently somewhere "between the times"—between the consummation of kingdom-mystery and the fullness of experiencing kingdom-reality.[8]

Real Presence

When we use the term "Real Presence" as Catholics, we do not speak metaphorically, symbolically, conceptually, abstractly, or figuratively, but we make a statement as to God's true and actual presence as "being real." Primarily, we would probably be thinking of the Sacrament of the Eucharist. In this Holy Sacrament, bread and wine truly and substantially become the body and blood of Jesus Christ through the power of the Holy Spirit. More will be said about this Sacrament in the final chapters of this book. However, because the Holy Spirit of Jesus Christ is really present and alive to us in other ways every day of our lives, this should not negate the real presence of God we might encounter in many other ways in "the sacrament of the present moment." Certainly, many of us have encountered the real presence of God in the silence of both our personal and communal prayer time, as well as in our reading the Bible as the Word of God come alive and the Holy Spirit being really present to us in the Sacred Scriptures. As both Augustine and Aquinas have told us, "Grace follows nature."[9] So, we encounter the real presence of God every day through some manner of God's created reality. We might find Him present in those who love us in our own family, in little children, in the poor or those suffering, in all of creation, in the neighbor, or the stranger. These and many other encounters of God's real presence will be discussed in several subsequent chapters of this book. In his most recent encyclical, *Dilexit Nos*, "He Loves Us," the late Pope Francis tells us:

> Jesus always finds a way to be present in your life, so that you can encounter him. (DN#38)[10]

Both the United Conference of Catholic Bishops in their doctrinal statements and the Catholic Catechism tell us that the presence of Christ in the Eucharist is called "real," not to exclude other types of His presence as if they could not be understood as "real." This is because the risen Christ manifests His real presence to His church in many ways, but it is most especially through the Sacrament of His body and blood (see Catholic Catechism no. 1374 and UCCB Basic Questions and Answers 2001).

There is more to encountering the real presence of God than what we might experience in the celebration of the Eucharist at Mass. The real presence of

God in the celebration of the Eucharist will be discussed in greater detail in the last two chapters of this book. Clearly, however, the real presence of Christ in the celebration of the Eucharist cannot be separated from all the other ways we might experience the real presence of God in all of reality. It is connected in every way. Finally, to repeat the title and the opening lyrics of the song we sing so often during the celebration of the Eucharist, we should always

> Look beyond the bread you eat, see your savior and your Lord/ Look beyond the cup you drink, see his love poured out as blood.[11,12,13]

Notes

1 Online from Henri Nouwen Society, Meditations, https://henrinouwen.org/meditations/god-is-a-god-of-the-present/

2 Ibid., Ch. 1, f 4.

3 St. Athanasius, found online at Brainyquote.com, https://www.brainyquote.com/search_results?x = 27&y = 3&q=athanasius

4 Raymond Brown, ed., *Jerome Biblical Commentary, Presence in the Old and New Testament* (Englewood Cliffs, NJ: Prentice Hall Pub., 1968), pp. 65–712.

5 "Omnipresence," *Encyclopedia Brittanica*, online, https://www.britannica.com/dictionary/omnipresent

6 "Sacramentality and the Principle of Sacramentality," ibid., Ch. 2, f. 4, see also ibid. Ch. 1, f 2.

7 J. P. De Caussade, S.J., *Sacrament of the Present Moment* (New York and San Francisco: Harper Pub., 1966), pp. 1–103.

8 "Transcendental Presence," ibid., Ch. 1, f 2, pp. 9–1199; see also ibid., Ch. 1, f 3, pp. 1734–51.

9 Ibid., Ch. 1, f 5, New Advent on "Grace and Nature," found online https://www.newadvent.org/fathers/1503.htm

10 Vatican Archives, Pope Francis, Dilexit Nos, found online, https://www.vatican.va/content/francesco/en/encyclicals/documents/20241024-enciclica-dilexit-nos.html

11 "Look Beyond," SJ BPBEC, online, https://sjbpbecmm.wordpress.com/songsheets/l/look-beyond /#:~:text=%2F%2F%3A%20LOOK%20BEYOND%20THE%20BREAD,LOVE%20POURED%20OUT%20AS%20BLOOD.

12 "Real Presence," Ibid., Ch. 1, f 2, pp. 826–30.

13 "Real Presence," Catechism of the Catholic Church, Second Edition, USCCB, United States Conference of Catholic Bishops, What We Believe, Library of the Vatican, CCC # 1374, 1994, found online, https://www.usccb.org/beliefs-and -teachings/what-we-believe/catechism/catechism-of-the-catholic-church

3

The Poor and Real Presence

The Anawim

In both the Old and New Testaments of the Bible, extreme poverty is seen to be a scandalous condition, an affront to human dignity, and contrary to the will of God. In the Old Testament, the poor person was first considered the *ani*, the weakened, bent-over, and burdened one. This gave rise subsequently to the poor being called the *anawim*, a Hebrew word which described the "poor and lowly ones" who remained faithful to God, especially during times of great difficulty. They were the humble, often silent, and oppressed people who became known as the *anawim* because they were the "faithful remnant of Yahweh" who were downcast, persecuted, and marginalized. Only the Lord and those who were faithful to God's covenant were the ones who were there for them and were given a mandate to speak for the *anawim*. Thus, these "lowly ones" showed their trust in God as being often present to them and in their midst by being faithful to His covenant as they prayed for God's deliverance from their oppression. The trust in God by the *anawim* was rooted from the beginning in the words of the Torah and later in the Pentateuch that Yahweh would be their protector and defender. The Israelites, who believed that God always heard the cry of the poor (Ps. 34), would then prayerfully open their hearts to the poor and lowly in their midst, believing that Yahweh was present and with them as well (Exod. 22:22–25; Deut. 15:7–11). Due to their suffering, lowly status, simple faith, humbleness of heart, and vulnerability, the *anawim* were seen by righteous Hebrews as the elect of Yahweh and as those who had to depend totally on the good Lord being present to them through His grace, kindness, goodness, generosity, and mercy. Those in Israel who considered themselves the righteous people of Yahweh wanted to follow God's example and recognized God's presence in the *anawim*. As we are told in several of the Psalms and through the prophets:

> The righteous cry out, the Lord hears, and he rescues them from all their afflictions. The Lord is close to the brokenhearted and saves those whose spirit is crushed (Ps. 34:18–19).
>
> ***
>
> Yahweh loves his people and he adorns the lowly with victory (Ps. 149:4).
>
> ***
>
> Blessed is the one who considers the poor! In the day of trouble, the Lord delivers him (Ps. 41:1).
>
> ***
>
> Yahweh hears the cry of the poor and his own who are in bonds he spurns not (Ps. 68:3).
>
> ***
>
> Whoever oppresses a poor man insults his Maker, but he who is generous to the needy honors him (Prov. 14:31).
>
> ***
>
> When the poor and needy seek water, and there is none, and their tongue is parched with thirst, I the Lord will answer them; I the God of Israel will not forsake them (Isa. 41:17).[1]

The Greek word to describe the poor person in the New Testament was *ptokos*. The care, concern, and love for the poor was a vital concern of the early Christian church as well (Mt. 25:31–46; Acts 6:1–7; Gal. 2:1–10; 6:10; Jas 1:27). In the New Testament, we find that Mary of Nazareth held a special place and was given a singular role among all the *anawim*. Her life was a life of quiet lowliness, humility, and faith-filled obedience to the Lord. Blessed was she among women. The Holy Spirit became a living presence in her womb and singled her out for a special place in God's salvific plan as God became a human being who was born as Jesus of Nazareth. She proclaimed in her Magnificat that the Almighty had done great things for her in being present to her in her lowliness, in contrast to God's dealings with the proud and lofty. Here is what Luke tells us:

> My soul proclaims the greatness of the Lord; my spirit rejoices in God my savior. For he has looked upon his handmaid's lowliness; behold, from now on will all ages call me blessed. The Mighty One has done great things for me and holy is his name. His mercy is from age to age to those who fear him. He has shown might with his arm, dispersed the arrogant of mind and heart. He has thrown down the rulers from their thrones but lifted up the lowly. The hungry he has filled with good things; the rich he has sent away empty. (Lk. 1:46–53)

The Almighty God, in the form of the infant baby Jesus, was born a human being. He was not born in a luxurious palace but a manger in a stable in Bethlehem; born into dire poverty. This made Jesus even more glorious in our eyes as He would become the richness of our souls and our beloved Lord.

Subsequently, after Mary gave birth to Jesus through the Holy Spirit, Jesus Christ will see Himself as being the Savior, defender, and deliverer of the *anawim* as He tells us in Luke's Gospel:

> The Spirit of the Lord is upon me because he has anointed me to preach the good news to the poor. He has sent me to proclaim release to the captives and recovery of sight to the blind, to set at liberty those who are oppressed, to proclaim the acceptable year of the Lord. (Lk. 4:18–19)

And because the Kingdom of God is in Jesus, He can tell the *anawim* most assuredly and with authority:

> The Kingdom of God is in your midst. (Lk. 17:21)

Mother Teresa of Calcutta had spent most of her earthly life among the poorest of the poor in the slums and ghettos of India. She very often spoke about recognizing the presence of our Lord in the disguise of the poor. She encouraged us often to realize that it is Christ we are actually serving when we help the poor, lowly, and oppressed of the world. In the words of Mother Teresa:

Seeking the face of God in everything, everyone, all the time, and his hand in every happening. This is what it means to be contemplative in the heart of the world. Seeing and adoring the presence of Jesus, especially in the lowly appearance of bread, and in the distressing disguise of the poor.... We must serve the poor devotedly because they allow us to serve Jesus, present in them.[2]

Also, the late Pope Francis takes his place among those in the church who take up the Old and New Testament Tradition and continue Jesus' role as defender of the *anawim*, who represent a real presence of the Lord in our own day and time. The Holy Father, in his pronouncements and through his social encyclicals, has told us:

In so many parts of the world there are children who have nothing to eat. That's not news, it seems normal. It cannot be this way! Yet these things become the norm: that some homeless people die of cold on the streets is not news. In contrast, a ten-point drop in the stock markets is a tragedy! A person dying is not news, but if the stock market drops ten points, it is a tragedy. Thus, people are disposed of as if they were trash.

Jesus teaches that poverty is not the result of fate, but a concrete sign pointing to his presence among us. We do not find him when and where we want, but see him in the lives of the poor, in their sufferings and needs; in the often-inhumane conditions in which they are forced to live.... The poor, always and everywhere, evangelize us, because they enable us to discover in new ways the true face of the Father.... It is necessary that we all let ourselves be evangelized by them. The new evangelization is an invitation to recognize the salvific power of their lives and to place them at the center of the Church's journey. We are called to discover Christ in them, to lend them our voice in their causes, but also to be their friends, to listen to them, to understand them and to welcome the mysterious wisdom that God wants to communicate to us through them.[3]

Christ is present and walking with the poor and lowly, but we just often miss Him. In so many ways, the people in our society seem to gravitate away from those who may need our loving kindness and help the most, but like the tendency of water (a sign and symbol of the Holy Spirit), Jesus Christ has a tendency to often seek out the lowest places. That is why we so often find Him present and embodied in the disguise of the poor person.

Solidarity with the Poor

Solidarity with the poor implies that there exists first an attitude of loving-kindness and justice toward the poor, lowly, and oppressed by those seeking it. It further implies that one values the basic rights and human dignity of all those in the community as individuals. It then enhances a spirit of unity whereby all are bonded with one another, including and especially the poorest, weakest, and most vulnerable in society. In addition to a spirit of unity, it emphasizes social charity, participation, interdependence, and mutual support. Some things that might mitigate against creating solidarity with the poorest, weakest, and most vulnerable are injustice, oppression, prejudice, intolerance, impatience, greed, exploitation, marginalization, and a basic lack of loving-kindness toward one's neighbor.

Solidarity with the poor and lowly is seen to be an intricate part of Jesus' mission to consummate the Kingdom of God on earth. Simply stated, Jesus preached the good news of the kingdom in word and deed, so the church must do the same. Jesus envisioned His mission to be the spreading of the good news among the hurting, weak, vulnerable, oppressed, the lowly, and the poor.

The church in the modern world, as the Body of Christ, continues to carry out Jesus' mission. For example, a few key documents generated at the Church Council Vatican II in 1962 were the Pastoral Constitution on the Church (*Gaudium et Spes*) and The Apostolate of the Laity (*Apostolicam Actuositatem*). The Pastoral Document opens with the following statement, and the Document on The Apostolate of the Laity follows:

> The joys and hopes, griefs and anxieties of the people of this age, especially those who are poor or in any way afflicted, those too are the joys and hopes, the griefs and anxieties of the followers of Christ.

> Assuming human nature, Christ bound the whole human race to himself as a family through a certain supernatural solidarity and established love as the mark of his disciples. Whereas there are people in need of food, clothing,

housing, medicine . . . wherever persons lack the facilities necessary for
living a truly human life . . . there Christian love should seek them out and
find them to console them.[4]

Why is it necessary for us as Christians to be in solidarity with the poor in
society? One of the primary reasons is because we must recognize that God is
not only present to them but also really present in them as well. Jesus Christ
has conferred on all human persons an inherent human dignity. This implies
that the poorest, weakest, and most vulnerable as members of society have
been given basic human rights and are entitled to Christian love and justice.

The principle of Solidarity is grounded in the Sacred Scriptures and a
long Tradition of Catholic Social Teaching.[5] In emphasizing loving-kindness
and justice, it is the glue that bonds us together as a community of persons,
including and especially the poorest, weakest, and most vulnerable. Jesus
Christ associates Himself in a real and present way with the poorest and
lowliest and is thus at the center of Christian Solidarity, which makes it more
powerful and mystical than mere fellowship.

It is when the poor are ignored, overlooked, or mistreated, whether
intentionally or unintentionally, that Christian Solidarity demands that some
persons in solidarity must speak for others who are rendered as silent and
have not been given a voice. Their cries of hunger, for basic human necessities,
human dignity, or the lifting of the yoke of oppression, may have largely
gone unheard by society. This is sometimes referred to as creating a need for
Christians in solidarity with the poor and oppressed to then make what is
termed a "preferential option for the poor."

Preferential Option for the Poor

"Preferential option for the poor" is solidly rooted in both the Old and
New Testament of the Bible as well as the Judeo-Christian Tradition (Exod.
22:20–26; Lev. 19:9–10; Job 34:20–28; Prov. 31:8–9; Isa. 25:4–5, 58: 5–7; Mt.
25:34–40; Lk. 4:16–21, 6: 20–23). It refers to a thread which runs throughout
the entire Bible describing how preference is given by God, the prophets, and

all righteous persons to the well-being of the poorest, most vulnerable, and powerless, who are close to the Lord. As Christians, we are called to look at the world from the perspective of those who are not only materially poor but also all those without a voice who are the most vulnerable or marginalized. Being in solidarity with the poor and lowly and in a sense, "preferring" to be among them is where Jesus was often found, and because God is most often found among the poorest and powerless, we are called to be in solidarity as their Christian brothers and sisters who are essentially "contemplatives in action." Jesus has promised us that He would always be a real presence and would be in our midst until the end of time, so the poor and lowly in many ways are a sacramental presence of God among us. In many ways, they become the voice of our God who speaks in silence. This also can be seen as arising in some ways from the Catholic experience of the Real Presence of Christ in the Eucharist. The Bible and the Tradition of the Catholic Church both further teach us:

> In every human being, above all in the least among us, one meets Christ himself (cf. Mt. 25:40).

> ***

> The Eucharist commits us to the poor. To receive in truth the body and blood of Christ given up for us, we must recognize Christ in the poorest, his brethren (CC137).

> ***

> The Eucharist commits us to the poor. To receive in truth the Body and Blood of Christ given up for us, we must recognize Christ in the poorest, his brethren (no. 1397).

If society at large does not somehow recognize a "preferential option for the poor," then by default, it makes a "preferential option for the status quo." Furthermore, it fails to understand that any social or economic question has a worldwide dimension, and any one part of society often affects other parts of society. This is not only true in society but most especially within the Body of Christ.

The resulting loss of human dignity and human rights of the poorest through oppression, marginalization, and powerlessness ends up wounding all of us.

The building of walls, whether physical or spiritual, to maintain inequality denies fundamental rights and keeps some poor and vulnerable persons from having a voice in society, and only heightens the oppression of the poorest among us. This also allows some persons to perceive others who live in extreme poverty as outcasts and as outright threats to security, democracy, and peace. This fuels efforts to ensure that some of societal poor, lowly, oppressed, and vulnerable are perpetually kept in proverbial or literal bondage in order to maintain a false sense of security, a pseudo-democracy, and an illusional peace. This peace is unsustainable because it has no foundation of love and is lacking in justice. Where there is no love or justice, there can be no peace; it becomes an illusion. In a different world ruled by love and concern for the common good of all humanity, including the poorest, rather than a quest for profit, peace would be possible. This would be the result of a more perfect justice among all persons who seek the presence of the Lord.

In a real way, the oppression of the poor and lowly ends up masking the percolating violence bubbling up like the inner core of a volcano beneath it. This is extreme violence in the sense that it seeks to continually oppress those who are the victims of the cycles of poverty and makes them not only poor, oppressed, and voiceless but in the worst-case scenario, they become increasingly unimportant, irrelevant, and ultimately, they become invisible.[6]

Pope Saint John Paul II has told us in his writings:

> The needs of the poor must be given preference to the wants and desires of the wealthy.[7]

The poor, lowly, and oppressed are part of those three billion people in our world who are needy, nameless, and ultimately depersonalized. They are those whose cries to God have been mostly drowned out and gone unheard by those of us who live our lives in a noisy, frenzied, chaotic, and bustling world that feeds off a consumerist society. We are like hamsters on a treadmill who live in a land of opportunity we call "the American dream," but the poor who do not participate are forced to live a nightmarish existence. We prohibit them, whether intentionally or unintentionally, from being any kind of full societal participants or even simply "American dreamers." Some of us would never dream, or even imagine for a second, that Jesus Christ would be in their midst, present and walking among them.

Because we live with an excess and more than what we need to live, others are forced to live with almost nothing at all. They are deprived of basic human needs which are theirs by right such as sustainable food, safe drinking water, health, shelter, and education. By focusing on our wants and desires instead of our needs, we ignore their human dignity, outright deny their basic human rights, and often even their very existence. We steadfastly refuse to hear their voices and ignore their cries because we are afraid to try to understand and accept the reality of their horrifying existence. As soon as we begin to hear their voices, we may have to attempt to bring them out of their oppression and into the whispers of our consciousness. This carries with it a recognition that it is we who, in some ways, have forced upon them their reality through our intended and unintended acts of social and economic oppression. Their cries of intense hunger, powerlessness, hopelessness, humiliation, and unfulfilled longing are not just cries heard by the Lord and those who currently recognize their terrible plight, but many of us actually believe that they represent the cries of the Holy Spirit of Jesus present in them. When the cries of the poor, oppressed, and lowly begin to be heard by more of us in society as well as within the Body of Christ, then more of us will say that we have heard that still small voice of the Lord.

Finally, it should be understood that our response to the poor, lowly, marginalized, and oppressed should not be material assistance alone. It should include efforts to make them increasingly self-reliant as full and productive participants because full participation is one of the pillars of any true democracy. It should also include advocacy for social and economic reform by speaking truth to power. This includes speaking out against unjust persons, institutions, and systems of government. It is then that the voice of the poor will begin to be heard not only by the Lord, who is ever-present to them as they are ever-present to Him, but by all of us who are listening with the ears of our hearts. It is in the Gospel of Matthew that Jesus tells us:

> Then the righteous will answer him and say, "Lord, when did we see you hungry and feed you, or thirsty and give you drink? When did we see you a stranger and welcome you, or naked and clothe you? When did we see you

ill or in prison, and visit you?" And the king will say to them in reply, "Amen, I say to you, whatever you did for one of these least of mine, you did for me." (Mt. 25: 37–40)

The Unborn

Whether called "babies" or "fetuses" in the world today, there are approximately seventy-five million unborn who are aborted each year. This equates to just under one-third of all pregnancies worldwide. According to the Guttmacher Institute and the Centers for Disease Control, there are currently just over one million abortions that occur in the United States each year. These unborn must be included among the poorest, lowliest, most vulnerable, and oppressed.[8]

The unborn are completely voiceless, helpless, and totally dependent. The only voices they have are the voices of those who are willing to speak for them. This is not to say that a woman should have no voice or that women should not speak for themselves or have those who choose to speak on their behalf regarding their basic human rights and reproductive freedoms. Of course, women should have these rights to exercise their own voice as well as to encourage others to speak for them. Everyone's basic human rights and freedom must be protected under the law.

This is only to say that, unlike most women, the unborn would be completely and totally silenced without the other voices who have chosen and will choose to speak for them. They are truly the *anawim* and among the poorest of the poor. They are totally innocent, defenseless, vulnerable, and completely reliant on the grace of God to stir the real presence of the Lord through enlivening His Holy Spirit within Christians and empowering some of us to become the voices of the unborn. Therefore, we should entrust the lives of all women and those who are unborn to Mary, the Mother of God, the Mother of Jesus, and the Mother of all who are alive in the Body of Christ, both born and unborn.

Finally, it is the Real Presence of Christ in the Eucharist that is the school in which we continue to learn to see God's face in the poorest and most vulnerable. As we enter into more of a real and present relationship in solidarity with Him, He then empowers us through His Holy Spirit to turn our gaze and look beyond the bread we eat. It is then that we see the light and shadows of His face really present and outlined in the faces of all people we encounter, but especially those excluded and most vulnerable, whom Christ still prefers to walk among today.

Notes

1 Ibid., Ch. 2, f 4 JBC, Sec. 14:11, 18:3, 10, 22:41, 48, 59:14

2 Online https://www.catholicapostolatecenter.org/blog/all-for-jesus-lessons-from-st-teresa-of-calcutta

3 Pope Francis, *Vatican Archives, Message of His Holiness, Pope Francis on the Fifth Day of the World Day of the Poor*, November 2021, https://www.vatican.va/content/francesco/en/messages/poveri/documents/20210613-messaggio-v-giornatamondiale-poveri-2021.html

4 Austin Flannery, ed., *Vatican Council II, Conciliar and Post Conciliar Documents* (Collegeville, Mn: Liturgical Press, 1975); *Constitution on the Church* (Gaudium et Spes) and *The Apostolate on the Laity* (Apostolicam Actuositatem).

5 Michael Hickey, *Catholic Social Teaching* (Lanham, Md.: Hamilton Books, 2018), Sec. One.

6 Ibid., Ch. 2, f 13, Catechism of the Catholic Church, UCCB, Preferential Option for the Poor, 1997, # pp. 2443–63, https://www.usccb.org/beliefs-and-teachings/what-we-believe/catholic-social-teaching/option-for-the-poor-and-vulnerable

7 His Holiness Pope John Paul II, Vatican Archives, Apostolic Encyclicals of John Paul II, online, https://www.vatican.va/content/john-paul-ii/en.html

8 Statistics of the Guttmacher Institute, found online, https://www.guttmacher.org/fact-sheet/10-points-consider-when-engaging-policy-debates-around-abortion

4

The Suffering and Real Presence

Non c'e rosa senza spine-*No rose without thorns[1]*

The above saying is an ancient Italian proverb I first learned in high school, and I have thought about its application several times in my own life, as well as in the lives of many family members and friends throughout the ensuing years. As it relates to this proverb, "Grace follows nature," as Thomas Aquinas has said in his *Summa*, and so perhaps we can deduce from that simple logic, "as in the natural, then so in the spiritual," . . . or put another way, if there truly is no rose without thorns, then perhaps there cannot be human life without the suffering that goes along with being human.[2]

Suffering often implies that one undergoes extreme pain, distress, and hardship that is part of it. Furthermore, to accept being human is to sometimes accept the suffering that is consistent with our humanity. Jesus was fully human-fully divine, so He certainly can identify with our experience of being human. He Himself encountered intense suffering and experienced death. Humans suffer and we die, and God allows this as part of His permissive divine will, but that's not the end of it, because God also gives us the virtuous graces of faith, hope, and love to believe that following any suffering and death, we will receive and experience new life along with the resurrected Jesus Christ. Jesus has promised that He will be with us always, whether in our suffering, death, or rising from the dead. We will be in the presence of Jesus Christ now and forever (Mt. 28:20).

Even though Jesus tells us that pain and suffering will be a part of our lives, He doesn't just mouth the words and then simply walk away or leave us to work things out on our own. In overcoming His own suffering and death,

He has overcome the world (Jn 16:33). This implies that any suffering, grief, hardship, trials, sickness, or tribulation we experience does not have to be meaningless but can be purpose-filled. In the end, we will have no more pain and suffering, and we can share the joy and peace of the risen Christ. All things will have worked for good as Christ will use our suffering as goodness (Rom. 8:28). The fact that our suffering along with Christ can bring about goodness at all is one of the great paradoxes of the Christian life. Sharing our suffering with Christ in prayer allows Him to be present to us in the power of the Holy Spirit as He gives us words of comfort, hope, healing, mercy, loving-kindness, and encouragement. He speaks to us in silence and empowers us to know He is there, present with us, and sharing our pain in this now-moment. The presence of Christ can change the way we face the starkness of reality each day. Without the real presence of Christ, we would be left to face our suffering, anxiety, trials, and discouragement on our own.

One of the most prominent theologians of our time who has written extensively on the mystery of suffering has been Dutch theologian, Fr. Edward Schillebeeckx, who tells us:

> Faith in God requires knowing that suffering is not meaningless or happens by chance. God is present in suffering, failure, and death. . . . As with Jesus on the cross, God never abandons the sufferer but is silently present. Then God's presence and power erupts, as God becomes manifest in the resurrection. The resurrection is God's corrective to the negativity of Jesus suffering and death.[3]

Suffering bonds us in solidarity with the cross of Christ in the Holy Spirit and allows us to not only participate in His suffering but also to enter into intimate communion with Him. In the exaltation of the cross of Christ as well as His resurrection and ascension, worldly wisdom is turned on its head. Suffering is ultimately turned into joy, death to life, and His seeming absence eventually will become His real presence anytime we receive the bread and wine of the Eucharistic Banquet. The resurrection of Jesus was a demonstrable act of God's love and God's answer to the question of Jesus' suffering. Following the resurrection, the ascension of Jesus into heaven is said to have taken place from the Mount of Olives (Acts 1:9–12; Lk. 24:50–51), but prior to the resurrection and the ascension of Jesus, which took place on the Mount of Olives, Jesus had to suffer on Mount Calvary (Lk. 23:33–56). Jesus' suffering was the first mountain He had to climb.

There are many followers of Jesus today who are climbing their own mountains of pain and suffering. No one invites suffering into their lives; it is always an uninvited and often unwelcome guest. But many believe that Jesus is present to them in the Holy Spirit as comforter, suffering along with them in their pain. Some who suffer can see their lives replicated in Jesus' life on earth. Jesus experienced not only torturous suffering and a brutal death on the cross but also rejection, sharp criticism, misunderstanding, false flattery, mocking, humiliation, grief, loss, betrayal, and intense pain. We can envision the presence of Jesus and His suffering by the existence of suffering occurring in our own lives. We can also have empathy for the lives of many others who are suffering today. Their suffering may be so real and present as to be unfolding before our very eyes. May Christ console them.

Some who suffer do so with joy. Since the time of the suffering and crucifixion of Jesus of Nazareth, many Christian saints in history have received what is called "the Stigmata." Some of the more recognizable ones have been St. Francis of Assisi, Catherine of Siena, and Padre Pio. They participated daily or often in replicating the physical and mental suffering associated with the wounds of Christ. These wounds came from the nail marks in the hands and feet, the spear thrust into His side, and the crown of thorns placed on His head. Most received wounds in the same locations as Christ's wounds. They also had the blood, scars, and pain to go along with their mutual suffering. In their suffering, Christ became very real and present to them. Pope St. John Paul II has said of them: "They are a living image of Christ, suffering and risen."[4] Even the Apostle Paul may have experienced something of a similar nature to the Stigmata in his journeys, as we read in his letter to the Galatians:

> From now on, let no one make troubles for me; for I bear the marks of Jesus on my body. (Gal. 6:17)

Paul is inferring that his body bears the scars of his apostolic labors such as floggings (Acts 16:22; 2 Cor. 11:25) and being stoned (Acts 14:19); these mark him as belonging to the Christ who suffered.

Suffering defies giving a logical or neat theological explanation for it, particularly the suffering of Jesus Christ, God's Son. Jesus is often referred to as "The Suffering Servant" (Isa. 53:12). We can talk about Jesus' suffering and other's suffering in the world as being redemptive or vicarious suffering, but I'm not sure that I understand the redemptive aspects of Jesus' suffering or universal suffering enough to try to explain it logically and rationally in this book. I don't want to simply quote Catholic doctrine that I really don't fully comprehend. The only thing I will say about it is to say that if Jesus Christ was not immune to suffering and pain, then Christians certainly wouldn't be immune to it either. We suffer along with the rest of the world. I also believe that Jesus' suffering and death did somehow bring about the forgiveness of my sins by God, the Father, and that alone is plenty enough "theology of redemptive suffering" for me to try to wrap my head around.

Suffering has been called one of the greatest mysteries of God. "God is love," as we are told in the Scriptures (1 Jn 4:7). Those who have the love of God in their hearts can and do suffer, as only a heart that loves and is loved is capable of being hurt, wounded, forsaken, or broken, so is the greatest mystery of God, suffering or is it love? In the end, we are not called to try to understand suffering or to explain it, but only to embrace it as the price of God's love for us, which is an even greater mystery. Jesus suffered and died before He was resurrected; that puts Jesus' presence right in the middle of all suffering and death as well as in the midst of all of God's unconditional love for humanity.

Our suffering may be of a physical, mental, emotional, financial, psychological, moral, social, or spiritual nature. It is when we are in the midst of our suffering and pain that we seek the most immediate relief from it. If that relief doesn't come even after begging God to remove the suffering and to take this cup from us—then we may not have any other better choice than to commune with Jesus. It is then that we may choose to enter into an "intimate communion of suffering" with one who knows by human experience what we are going through. In his Apostolic Letter, *Salvifici Doloris*, "Salvific Suffering," Pope John Paul II tells us:

Christ drew close to the world of suffering through taking this suffering upon his very self. . . . Christ through his own salvific suffering is very much present in every human suffering and can act from within that suffering by the powers of his consoling Spirit. (16) (26)[5]

For most Christians, it is when our suffering is so intense that Jesus can often be the most present to us, as our most passionate prayers are usually when we are in the most pain. At that time, our praying becomes a genuine cry of the heart. Jesus will often meet and be present to us at our lowest point, where we are experiencing the most weakness, despair, and desperation. When we are suffering ourselves or someone we love is suffering, telling ourselves or someone we love that Jesus is there with us and present to us may not simply make that intense pain and distress disappear. We can only be present to others along with Jesus at that time.

Many years ago, my first Bible study teacher, Nina Pension, told a touching story in a Bible study class. The story has meant more and more to me through the years. It's still the little boy in me that likes to hear stories that have a moral. I hope you like this kind of story as well.

The Story of the Little Child in the Crib

As momma lay her little child down and put her in the crib for the night, she hugged her daughter lovingly, kissed her tenderly, and said, "You can go to sleep now precious because Jesus is right here and present in your room with you."

The child lay down, and a few minutes later, the little girl stood up in the crib, crying and yelling for her momma. The mother came back into the room and said once again, "Go to sleep dear; I told you . . . Jesus is right here in the room with you."

The child lay down again, and in less than a minute later was screaming and hollering at the top of her lungs for her momma. The mother came back into the room once more, and this time, the little child stood up in the crib, grabbed her mother's hand tightly, and said, "Mommy, I know Jesus is right here in the room with me but stay here with me for a little while because right now, I just need someone with a little skin on them."[6]

The moral of this story is that we can be present to Jesus in the Holy Spirit among us by being present to other people in their suffering, pain, or distress. Sometimes we can be for them "Jesus in the skin."

Finally, we should realize that there is something far worse than our personal suffering or the suffering of those we love, and that is going through it without realizing that the Lord is really present and there with us. Suffering without belief in God's presence among us must be unbearable for anyone in that situation. Any relief from the pain can then only be a temporary fix and some form of drugged or self-medicated alternative that never lasts. Suffering with the Lord being present to us and in us through the power of the Holy Spirit has to be far more bearable than the alternative for those without faith. Without faith, there is no hope that the suffering will somehow end for us in eternal love. It is tantamount to having a life filled with only thorns while lacking the scent-filled presence of the rose.

Notes

1 "No Rose without Thorns," Italian Proverb found in the Italian Dictionary online, https://en.bab.la/dictionary/italian-english/non-c-%C3%A8-rosa-senza-spine #google_vignette

2 Ibid., Ch. 1, f 5, Aquinas, *Summa Theologica*, Questions, 109, 110, 11, 112, New Advent Online, https://www.newadvent.org/summa/2109.htm

3 E. Schillebeeckx, "Suffering in the Theology of Edward Schillebeeckx," *Theological Studies* 60, no. 3 (1999), found online at https://theologicalstudies.net/wp-content/ uploads/2022/08/60.3.4.pdf

4 "Stigmata," Catholic Education Resource Center, https://catholiceducation.org/en /culture/what-is-the-stigmata.html; see also https://www.vatican.va/content/john -paul-ii/en/encyclicals.index.html

5 His Holiness John Paul II, Vatican Archives, Salvifici Doloris, 1984, https://www .vatican.va/content/john-paul-ii/en/apost_letters/1984/documents/hf_jp-ii_apl _11021984_salvifici-doloris.html

6 Nina Pension, *Story told at Our Lady of the Assumption Church* (Lynnfield, MA: Bible Study, 1976).

5

The Children and Real Presence

As the opening lyric of that old Sunday School song goes, "Jesus loves the little children, all the children of the world."[1] This simple song calls attention to the childlike faith that is an example of the innocence, trust, simplicity, and humility necessary to become a true follower of Jesus Christ.

In the Gospels, very often children were being brought to Jesus, probably by their parents, to be blessed by Him. The disciples, not wanting Jesus to be bothered by this interruption, rebuked them and tried to turn the people and their children away. In those days, Jewish people did not romanticize having children. There were no kids' Reebok Weeboks to wear, Chuck E. Cheese Pizza parlors to celebrate birthdays, Disney World Castles to visit, or Barbie dolls to play with. Instead, children were thought to be somewhat insignificant, irrelevant, and lacking in power or honor. As far as not recognizing them, Jesus wouldn't have it, He would call the children into His midst, lay His hands on the little ones, and bless them, saying:

> Let the children come to me and do not prevent them; for the Kingdom of God belongs to such as these. Amen, I say to you, whoever does not accept the Kingdom of God like a child will not enter it. (Lk. 18:16–17)

The Gospel writer, Luke, inserts this verse on children (above) to intentionally give us a stark contrast to the attitudes of the Pharisee in the preceding episode (see Lk. 18:9–14) and then that of the wealthy official in the verses immediately following this verse on children (see Lk. 18:18–23). His intention appears to be to show us that the kingdom is not simply for the privileged or the powerful. The kingdom is also not for those who think that they can lay claim to God's favor by their own merit. That should not be the "kingdom attitude." The presence of the kingdom is within Jesus, so the attitude of any disciple who seeks out the presence of Jesus Christ and wants to enter the Kingdom of God should be marked by the receptivity and trustful dependence characteristic of the humble and innocent child. Children have simple and pure hearts; they are often gentle, peaceable, vulnerable, curiously teachable, and they love unconditionally. Where they are present, Jesus can be found in their midst. The presence of children can lead us and show us the way to where Jesus and the Kingdom of God are made manifest and really present today in our midst.

In showing the way to the Kingdom of God where He is present, Jesus turns things upside down and stands them on their head. It's not for the privileged, the powerful, the wealthy, or the social and cultural elite. The kingdom includes those who would usually have been excluded—not only children but the poor, the humble, immigrants, prostitutes, and tax collectors, the foreigners and strangers, the marginalized, powerless, and meek, those considered unimportant or irrelevant, the literal and metaphorical lepers, the outcasts, and all the rest of the so-called nobodies of this world. Jesus wants them to know that the Kingdom of God is in their midst, as it is present within Him.

To reinforce this reality, Jesus, in another place with different words, will say something similar:

> I give praise to you Father, Lord of heaven and earth, for although you have hidden these things from the wise and the learned, you have revealed them to the merest children. (Mt. 11:25)

The door to the Kingdom of God is opened for those who receive Jesus' message with the ears of their hearts and the innocence, simplicity, and helpless dependence of a little child. The door is closed to those who are clever in their own estimation—the prideful and puffed-up know-it-alls who don't even realize how smug and arrogant they are. The veil that covers the entrance is lifted only for those who receive Jesus' kingdom-presence with childlike awe and wonder. They realize they are simply dependent on the grace of God and not their own merit or superior worldly wisdom as "somebodies."

St Therese of Lisieux, the "little flower," was someone who trusted in the unconditional love of God like a small child. St. Therese eventually realized that her littleness was the very source and foundation of her relationship with God. She trusted the Lord with the complete innocence, simplicity, confidence, and dependence of a little child. In fact, as a Carmelite sister, her spirituality has been called "the little way of spiritual childhood." In her autobiography, *Story of a Soul*, St. Therese would tell us:

> What matters in life, is not great deeds, but great love. . . . Jesus has shown me that the only way that leads to the fire of divine love is that of a little child who, full of trust, falls asleep in its father's arms.[2]

Therese saw herself as "the Little Flower of Jesus" because she never imagined herself as one of the beautiful and elegant roses. She was just like a small, simple wildflower in the Lord's garden, unnoticed by the wider world yet still growing and giving glory to God. She had a simple, childlike focus throughout her short life and believed in always doing the ordinary with extraordinary love. St. Therese truly had the "kingdom-attitude" and the awe-filled wonder of a little child.

It should be said that in describing the kingdom attitude in children, and how the kingdom is present in them, Jesus is talking more about faith, trust, innocence, humility, and helpless dependence that small children might naturally possess. He is in no way presenting all the (not so terrific) qualities that children might also have. We know children are not always simply sweet and lovable: they can throw temper tantrums and are occasionally irascible. When they don't get their way, children can sometimes stomp their feet and whine until they do. Children can occasionally act more like "little weeds" than "little flowers." They can be stubborn, inconsolable, and uncontrollable, just to name a few. Like us, children are "imperfect saints," but they are housed in smaller bodies. Perhaps this is why in showing children to be the exemplary model for the kingdom attitude, Jesus will qualify it by adding the words, "to such as these." Jesus didn't want us to think He meant that all children had the qualities of little perfect cherubic angels flying around the kingdom; these were some natural qualities children possess because they were simply children that made them the best example He could possibly use.

In our church today, in the Sacrament of Baptism, children are first joined to the priesthood of Jesus Christ and become members of the church as the Body of Christ on earth. That anointing is then strengthened in the Sacrament of Confirmation. The Sacrament of the Eucharist will renew the covenant with Christ, who is real and present, just as He was real and present when the child received the Sacraments of Baptism and Confirmation. Each additional reception of the repeated Sacrament of the Eucharist will recall the fullness of the Holy Spirit present in all three of these Sacramental encounters with Christ.[3]

When we become adults, we can't fit any longer in the tiny body of a little child, but our attitude can still be an uncomplicated kingdom attitude that retains the simple faith in Jesus. It is the renowned Catholic Bishop, theologian, and evangelist, Fr. Robert Barron, who first credits St. Thomas Aquinas for the reason he became a priest. He goes on to say that the Lord reminds us that the mind can easily become arrogant and self-important. Then, in speaking of the tremendous effect that Aquinas, who compiled the *Summa Theologica*, had on his life, he tells us:

> Even though Thomas Aquinas was one of the greatest geniuses who ever lived, he still had by all accounts, the soul of a little innocent child.[4]

Teaching Children about the Real Presence

Child development specialists tell us that the prefrontal cortex of a child's brain, responsible for critical thinking, doesn't fully develop until the teenage years. At the younger ages of seven or eight years old, they do not have abstract or conceptual thinking skills. They think primarily in terms of black and white without many gray areas. Children also get bored very easily, but if they can grasp being in the real presence of Jesus Christ in the Sacrament of the Eucharist and what that means, they could never be bored. Children generally celebrate the Sacrament of their First Communion before the fourth grade, and most often when they are about the age of seven or eight years old. When they are this age, they usually can see and understand things in concrete, actual, and factual terms. They not only have some difficulty wrapping their heads around gray areas but also in getting their minds to think in the abstract. At this age, it's difficult for them to try to grasp figurative terms or symbolism or to understand what exactly a metaphor is. This can work as something positive in their religious education formation as we try to explain the real presence of Christ in plain and simple terms. Concrete and nonfigurative terms are the best and only way we can explain the real presence of Jesus Christ, considering that when Jesus instituted the Sacrament of the Eucharist, we believe that He wasn't speaking in symbolic terms or using metaphorical language. He was telling believers of all ages that the bread and wine were being transformed (transubstantiated) into His body and blood. He told disciples in strictly black-and-white terms that "his body was real food, and his blood was real drink."

It could be a challenge to try to explain why Jesus would come to us as food in the bread and wine of the Eucharist. It doesn't have to be. Perhaps the best way is to meet it head-on and simply explain that, when we celebrate the Eucharist, God changes the bread and wine so that they become Jesus Himself. It still looks and tastes like bread and wine, but it is really Jesus coming into your body and soul as bread and wine. A child seven or eight years old can understand this. Unfortunately, it's many adults that seem to have developed a problem grasping this. It is often just too literal and unexaggerated for grown-ups. It's supposed to be understood as simply the unvarnished truth because it's distinctly factual. It's not figurative, metaphorical, or symbolic language. Is it any wonder why Jesus told us that we must become like little children to enter the Kingdom of God?[5]

He comes in the form of bread to remind us of His Body, and the form of wine to remind us of His blood. We can explain why Jesus gives Himself as bread and wine by telling children that Jesus wants to be very real and present to them and to become very close to them. He seeks to become a very part of them, to nourish them, and for children to become a very part of Him. The Eucharist helps us to form our lives through the bread and wine to become more like Jesus in how we live.

Similar to husband-wife and parent-child relationships, all relationships are nourished and strengthened by shared and expressed love, and by the quality of our being lovingly present to each other. Our relationship with Jesus is not totally unlike that. Although we might not encounter Jesus in exactly the same way as we do other people, He does offer us a chance to have a relationship with Him through a mutuality of love and presence. The Real Presence of

Christ in the Eucharist allows children to more fully experience Jesus' greatest gift to them—the reality of the gift of Himself in the present now-moment.

Children need to be assured that God comes to us in a special way in the Holy Communion and that His real presence to each child is in the Holy Spirit, so what is happening is much more than what they are seeing. It is an experience of the Holy Spirit inside them, transforming them, and making them a more holy and loving child—and as they grow older, an even better man or woman. The change of the bread and wine into Jesus' body and blood in the Sacrament of the Eucharist is bringing about a change in them because Jesus loves them and will continue to love them throughout their whole lives. The body and blood of Christ, changed from bread and wine, are simply changing them into a child of Christ and not just their mommy and daddy's child. Why? Because Christ is at the center of each life within the family—mom's, dad's, and now yours as well. This makes our family become more and more a part of God's family as it's united with the family of the Trinity: Father, Son, and Holy Spirit.

Notes

1 "Jesus Loves the Little Children," written and composed by C. Herbert Woolston, Songs of Zion, no. 26, in 1913 online, https://www.umcdiscipleship.org/articles/history-of-hymns-jesus-loves-the-little-children

2 St Therese of Lisieux, Story of a Soul, online, https://benedictinesofdivinewill.org/uploads/3/4/3/2/34324596/story-of-a-soul.pdf

3 Ibid., Ch. 2, f 13, CCC #, pp. 1210–690.

4 Bishop Robert Barron, Sermons, "You Have Revealed to the Merest Children," *Word on Fire*, 2002, online video, https://www.wordonfire.org/videos/sermons/you-have-revealed-to-the-merest-children/

5 Ibid., Ch. 1, f 2, pp. 826–30, see also Ibid., Ch. 2, f 13, CCC #, pp. 1374–81.

6

The Prisoner, the Stranger, and Real Presence

The Lord sets prisoners free . . . protects strangers (Ps. 146:7, 9).

God is in everyone and exists anywhere and everywhere. God hides Himself to allow us to discover Him under every kind of masterful disguise, including masquerading in the unlikely form of the prisoner or stranger. God chooses who and what many people shun, reject, overlook, despise, ignore, or exclude to reveal His presence.

The Prisoner

In the Old Testament of the Bible, we find many examples of the Lord's presence through the people who are either visiting or caring for prisoners or welcoming and protecting strangers. This occurs particularly in many of the Psalms (e.g., Pss. 68, 69, 79, 142, 146). In the New Testament, when Jesus begins His public ministry, He says He has come "to proclaim release to the captives" (Lk. 4:16–21). The language is even more powerful as Jesus will tell us that with both prisoners and strangers, when we cared for, protected, or visited them, it was Him. His transcendent presence is embodied in both the prisoner and the stranger. We see this in the Gospel of Matthew, for example:

> For I was hungry, and you gave me food, I was thirsty, and you gave me drink, a stranger and you welcomed me, naked and you clothed me, ill and you cared for me, in prison and you visited me. (Mt. 25:35–36)

The risen Christ became a real presence to the Apostle Paul, beginning with his conversion from Saul to Paul on the Damascus Road. Along with the twelve

Apostles, Paul was used as a vital instrument of Jesus Christ in spreading the good news throughout the world of that time. Today, we might refer to Paul as a "repeat offender," as he spent much time in prison in almost every Christian community he founded. He received many gifts from these communities while in prison and more than a few personal visits from his fellow Christians during incarceration for his missionary activity. We know he was imprisoned on at least three occasions in Philippi (Phil. 1:7, 13, 17; 2:25, 4:14, 18; Col. 3:13, 18), also in Caesarea and Rome (Acts 24:27, 28:16–31) and possibly Ephesus (Eph. 3:1; 4:1; 6:20).

Today, in the abyss of loneliness we call "the prison system," it is not just the prisoners who end up suffering, but all of us. If Christ identifies Himself with the prisoner, whatever is done to a prisoner is done to Christ. When a prisoner is locked away and isolated, Christ is locked away in isolation. When we separate from those in prison, in certain ways, we separate ourselves from Christ. Taking action to become "captivated" by Jesus Christ and serving those who are incarcerated lets us know that in many ways, we are serving Christ Himself.

Jesus always sought out those who were the most excluded from the surrounding culture and society: the poor and lowly, the women and children, the tax collectors, prostitutes, slaves, lepers, as well as the prisoners and the strangers who were otherwise powerless. There was no sort of organized prison ministry in the Jewish or Roman culture of that time, yet visiting prisoners quickly became a practice of presence for which the early church became known. From the very start of Jesus' ministry, beginning with the likes of John the Baptist and the Apostle Paul, Christians came to see prison ministry as the proper response to Jesus' statement about the blessed ones who would be inheriting "the kingdom prepared for you since the creation of the world. For . . . I was in prison, and you came to visit me" (see Mt. 25:35–36 above).

In the Middle Ages, St. Peter Claver,[1] a Catalonian Jesuit, declared himself to be "the slave of the Africans" and went to Colombia, South America, as a missionary to the imprisoned slaves working in the mines and on farms. He knew he could not offer them their freedom but was able to give them the presence of Christ by showing them loving-kindness, mercy, and healing from their sense of isolation, abandonment, and helplessness. In many small ways, he attempted to restore their personhood by helping them to regain their stolen human dignity.

Today, two of the world's largest prison ministries, "Prison Fellowship" founded by the late Chuck Colson and the "Catholic Prison Ministry,"[2] grew out of the practice of presence begun by Jesus and continued in His name by the early Christian church. Thanks to these ministries and others like them today, prisoners would no longer be separated from a priestly and ministerial presence, care, concern, advocacy, frequent prison visits, and particularly those who would offer prisoners a Biblical and Sacramental worldview. These ministries and other prison fellowships like them do make a tremendous difference in the lives of those who are incarcerated. Prisoners often cling helplessly to Jesus' promise of His Holy Spirit presence because they have few other options. The personal presence someone offers to one who is imprisoned can possibly help to liberate them, first from the inside out. By becoming a real and Godly presence to the incarcerated, we recognize them as children of God and bequeath a true personhood to them by restoring their human dignity. In the end, our solidarity with them is what might help to determine their eternal destiny as well as our own. May the Holy Spirit bless and support all those personally, ministerially, or financially involved in prison outreaches today.

The United States comprises only 5 percent of the world's population, yet we imprison 25 percent of the world's prisoners. We incarcerate more of our citizens than any other nation—currently just under two million people. While nearly 450,000 Americans are released from correctional facilities annually, two-thirds are rearrested within three years, and 71 percent of all prisoners released end up back in prison at some other point in their lives. Each year, our country spends over $80 billion to incarcerate and reincarcerate prisoners.[3] Beyond the financial impact on our tax-paying citizens, the seemingly nonstop cycle of crime and incarceration produces broken relationships, victimization, despair, and instability, impacting families and communities across the nation. What we are currently doing in simply locking up prisoners, has never been able to stem this flow of an increased incarceration explosion or come close to fixing the problems. There has got to be a better way.

The answer lies in the changed hearts of both those who are incarcerated and the attitude toward them that exists in the hearts of the wider population.

Only the presence of Jesus Christ through the power of His Holy Spirit can do that by creating more love, caring, and concern, and a change in all hearts. The alternative of incarceration and reincarceration will eventually reach a point where we will not be able to build prisons fast enough to contain all the prisoners, or we will exhaust the funds that render us financially able to do so. Prisoners especially need an intervention of love. In the book of Hebrews, the writer tells us what this kind of love might look like, saying:

> Remember those who are in prison, as though you were in prison with them; those who are being tortured as though you yourselves were being tortured. (Heb. 13:3)

In other words, we need to be the presence of Christ to them, to not only remember them but to identify with them and imagine ourselves as being one of them. The Bible tells us that love is all there is in the end. The presence of love is in many ways the real presence and power of the Holy Spirit. Come Holy Spirit!

The Stranger

When a stranger comes, Christ comes.[4]

—St. Benedict

"Stranger" commonly translates the Hebrew word *ger*, which means a resident alien, foreigner, or sojourner. In a society and culture that had defined boundaries for tribes and nations, such "strangers" had no civic, land, or familial rights. Welcoming and entertaining the presence of strangers actually began as far back as Father Abraham entertaining three strangers as guests (Gen. 18:1–33). However, since the earliest times, beginning in the Pentateuch and throughout the Old Testament (Lev. 19:33–34, Deut. 1:16, 10:17–19; 14:28–29, 16:11–14, Jer. 7:6), the Israelites were cautioned on how to interact with strangers and why. They were reminded time and again by the Lord that they needed to be welcoming and hospitable to strangers because they, themselves, had been in the same situation, being strangers and aliens in the land of Egypt:

You shall not oppress a resident alien; you well know how it feels to be an alien, since you were once aliens yourselves in the land of Egypt. . . . For six days you may do your work, but on the seventh day you must rest that your ox and your donkey may have rest, and that the son of your maidservant and the resident alien may be refreshed. Give heed to all that I have told you. (Exod. 23:9, 12–13)

In the New Testament, as was stated earlier, in the Gospel of Matthew 25:35, Jesus cautions His disciples and followers that the way they welcomed and cared for strangers was in effect the way they welcomed, cared for, and treated Him. This welcoming of strangers and being hospitable toward them continued into the mission and ministry of the early Christian church community. The presence of a stranger could occasionally be seen as a transcendental surrogate for the presence of an angel. For example, we find this statement in the book of Hebrews:

Do not forget to show hospitality to strangers, for by doing so some people have shown hospitality to angels without knowing it. (Heb. 13:2)

In this passage, as well as several others (e.g., Rom. 12:13; 1 Pet. 4:9; 3 Jn 1:5), the habit of showing hospitality to all, but especially to strangers, was seen as the proper attitude and was an important characteristic of those Christian disciples who sought to follow Jesus. It was practiced by showing loving-kindness and care to the stranger, as well as having a favorable disposition toward their presence. When we practice hospitality, strangers will be quick to recognize our willingness to provide genuine care in showing them Christian love as well as having a favorable disposition to their presence by manifesting the presence of Christ through the Holy Spirit. Hospitality awakens in us the simple, yet powerful perception, that another person whom we do not recognize is in our presence. In doing this, we recognize the presence of Christ. The early Christian church was to support and offer hospitality to one another, but especially to those strangers who had come to join them in worship.[5]

Today, Christ the stranger might approach us as a Buddhist, a Jew, a Muslim, an old woman, a homeless beggar, a black-hooded teenager, a special needs child, a bald gay man, or just simply someone who might be asking for directions. Our God is often a God of surprises, whose grace-filled plan for our lives is never what we expect. Seeing Christ among us as the stranger in our midst means seeing Christ in those whom we would never expect to see Him. We need to remember that whoever that stranger is, there will be no strangers in heaven. We will all know each other as one blessed family of God in Christ, and love each other just as soon as we meet.

The importance of showing hospitality and welcoming strangers is really brought to light in the Emmaus Road experience as told by the Gospel writer Luke, as we find two disciples of Jesus just talking while walking on the way:

> While they were talking and discussing, Jesus himself came near and went with them, but their eyes were kept from recognizing him. And he said to them, "What are you discussing with each other while you walk along?" (Lk. 24: 16, 17)

Whatever the two disciples might have felt about being approached by a total stranger, Jesus didn't seem to have any reluctance about joining them and including Himself in their conversation. In some ways, it might have seemed rude and intrusive, but if the two disciples had refused to welcome that stranger into their walk and talk, they would have missed the whole Eucharistic encounter with Jesus! Jesus has told us that when we welcome and show hospitality to strangers, we are welcoming Christ Himself. This is exactly what happened to the two disciples who had the experience on the Emmaus Road. They merely acted in faith by welcoming the stranger into their walk and their intimate one-on-one conversation, and then, lo and behold, a little later, they both discovered it was Christ Himself as

> They recognized him in the breaking of the bread. (Lk. 24:30)

Notes

1   "St. Peter Claver," Lotha, G. et al., *The Editors of Encyclopedia Brittanica*, 1999, online, https://www.britannica.com/biography/Saint-Peter-Claver/additional -info

2   Prison Fellowship Ministry, founded by Chuck Colson, Merrifield, Va., *Catholic Prison Ministries*, 409–411 Olive St., Scranton, Pa.

3 Statistics from Prison Fellowship Ministry, "What We Do—Why Help Prisoners Icon," online, https://www.prisonfellowship.org/why-help-prisoners/?utm_source =google&utm_medium=cpc&utm_campaign

4 St. Benedict, quote from Ch. 53, Rule of St. Benedict, *Reception of Guests*, online, https://christdesert.org/rule-of-st-benedict/chapter-53-the-reception-of-guests/

5 M. Hickey, *Get Goodness, Virtue is the Power to do Good*, "Hospitality," (Lanham, MD: University Press, 2005).

7

Creation and Real Presence

Bereshit bara Elohim et hashamayim ve'et ha'aretz, (Hb.)—In the beginning God created the heavens and the earth (Gen. 1:1).

I have always been awestruck by the fact that the Creator of the entire universe, God Almighty, chose to become a tiny human child in Mary's womb and that at one time in the ongoing history of the world, Jesus' entire universe was the Blessed Mother's womb. Isn't it magnificent to just imagine that even our Lord and Savior, Jesus Christ, the King of Glory, was once a tiny baby in the womb of His mother, Mary? He was comforted by hearing her heartbeat and being nourished only by an attachment to her umbilical cord. Thus, in many ways, creation was recreated and took the form of this tiny human child who was, is, and always will show us the way to envisioning the ever-changing real presence of God.

Creation can be a window into the divine presence. We know that we can hear God speaking to us through His living Word in the Bible and experience His real presence in the Eucharist; however, the divine presence of God can also be seen, heard, touched, and experienced through His creation and the natural world around us. We can see God in the springtime buds or flowers of the field, hear God in the wind, smell God in the sea, taste God in the fruit of the land, and touch God by holding a small child. This is sometimes referred to as a "theophany" or "epiphany," which is a visible manifestation of the divine presence in an observable and tangible encounter with God through His created world. In this way, the divine gives us insight into His real presence.[1] The Catholic Catechism tells us that

God transcends creation and is present to it. . . . God is present to his creatures inmost being. (CCC#300)[2]

It was Thomas Aquinas in his *Summa* who told us that "grace follows nature," or "grace presupposes nature." We might extend this theological understanding to say that creation is really "graced nature." This would further imply that everything in nature is significant, no matter how seemingly insignificant or small. Therefore, we should not ignore or minimize the fact that in creation, ordinary natural things can show us much sacramentally about the real presence of God.[3]

Taking the word "sacrament" in its broadest sense as a visible sign of something invisible or sacred and hidden, we could say that the whole natural world is a vast sacramental system in that many material things are unto humankind, the signs of things spiritual and sacred. The real presence of God can often be revealed in many natural and visible created realities, but God will always remain more than that. Anything else is not God but merely an idol. Many things in creation are imbued with the hidden real presence of God. Therefore, they can be a sign of grace or a natural signal of transcendence. If all of nature can be imbued with the mysterious and hidden presence of God, this would necessarily imply that God can choose to become really present to us and reveal Godself to us throughout creation in other people, events, animals, objects, the earth and universe around us, or for that matter, anything natural, material, tangible, visible, or as an event occurring in history. Because of the principle of sacramentality, all of creation can have a grace-filled hidden character. The Holy Mystery that is God can be seen in virtually everyone and everything all around us in creation.[4]

St. Francis of Assisi is a good example of someone who experienced this. St. Francis saw God mysteriously reflected in the sun, moon, and stars. He saw God in animals as well as everyone and everything around him. If all that is visible and material in the natural world around us can convey the mystery of a hidden God, then that should say to us that all created reality has a sacramental and mysterious character. This should further imply that all visible or invisible created reality can be mediated to us by the unveiling of its meaning by the Holy Spirit.

When we look at creation, we see a continuous transformation and development from a simple and often hidden program to a more intricate, developed, complex, and "glorious" one. For example, a flower from a tiny seedling or a fully grown tree emerging from the program lying within its respective seed involves a mystery in that unless a seed dies, it cannot produce life. When the shell of the seed becomes soft in the ground and is nourished with water and warmed by the sun, it somehow germinates, puts forth roots, and then transforms as it sprouts out of the earth. After that, it grows and produces fruit and many more seeds. Closer to home, a fully developed multitrillion celled human person emerges from a fertilized egg and embryo. Would it then be a stretch to possibly envision a new and glorified body emerging from a dead one?

In the Gospels, Jesus often utilized examples from the natural world to show how the presence of God could be seen in created reality all around us. In John's Gospel, for instance, Jesus will give the disciples this example from the natural world as a foreshadowing of His own death and resurrection:

> Amen, amen, I say to you, unless a grain of wheat falls to the ground and dies, it remains just a grain of wheat; but if it dies, it produces much fruit. (Jn 12:24)

All the disciples would be able to comprehend at that time was the natural sense that Jesus was using as an example from agriculture of how a seed dies, is buried in the ground, and then bears fruit. This had been the case for all to see as far back as people could remember. The disciples just couldn't wrap their heads around how that related to Jesus' imminent crucifixion, death, burial, and resurrection. Soon, they would see for themselves and be able to grasp exactly what Jesus had been talking about.

The Apostle Paul also draws some wonderful comparisons from creation, beginning with a tiny seed and then further discussing all dying and a glorious bodily resurrection in first Corinthians:

> But someone may say, "How are the dead raised? With what kind of body will they come back ?" You fool! What you sow is not brought to life unless it dies. And what you sow is not the body that is to be but a bare kernel of wheat, perhaps, or of some other kind; but God gives it a body as he chooses,

and to each of the seeds its own body. Not all flesh is the same, but there is one kind for human beings, another kind of flesh for animals, another kind of flesh for birds, and another for fish. There are both heavenly bodies and earthly bodies, but the brightness of the heavenly is one kind and that of the earthly another. The brightness of the sun is one kind, the brightness of the moon another, and the brightness of the stars another. Star differs from star in brightness. So also, is the resurrection of the dead. It is sown corruptible; it is raised incorruptible. It is sown dishonorable; it is raised glorious. It is sown weak; it is raised powerful. It is sown a natural body; it is raised a spiritual body. If there is a natural body, there is also a spiritual one. (1 Cor. 15: 35–44)

If we look at the natural world around us more closely, we will also see many more examples of how the real presence of the Creator can be seen in creation. The sun rises each morning to bring light as the new day follows night, and this cycle has been occurring since time began. In looking at the seasons, spring and summer always follow the dead of winter. Leaves on trees turn brown and die off in the fall and winter, and then, as tiny buds appear, they turn a vibrant green in spring, while in the summer, much fruit is borne. Following that, in the fall, the dying process begins all over again. In nature, the cycle of rising unto new life continually follows after the process of death and dying.

In the insect world, we see the life cycle of the creeping earthbound caterpillar as it willingly encases itself in its own self-made tomb and completely dissolves, becoming a chrysalis. From this inglorious tomb emerges the beautifully new and more glorious body of the emergent butterfly. The rebirth of this new creation is capable of higher movements and increased possibilities that were impossible in its earthbound original state of being. Life goes on in a new and transformed state. The universe around us can give us so many examples of how God the Father uses the world of "Mother Nature" to point the way to finding the real presence of the Creator throughout creation.

Water

Water is a key natural resource that is essential for all created life on earth. In fact, even the bodies of human beings are made up of 60 percent water;

55 percent of our blood is plasma, which is 90 percent water. Since life on earth began, water has been a natural symbol of cleansing, purifying, rebirth, and renewal. Some of the unique characteristics of water are that it has the ability to cleanse itself of discoloration and dirt and become pure and clean once again. In addition to human beings cleansing themselves physically, water is also seen as a means of spiritual rebirth and renewal. Additionally, it is a natural sign of dying and rising to new life in many world religions, including Christianity. Water is used in many baptismal rituals. In the Scriptures, water is one of the natural symbols for the Holy Spirit. Many people bathe in holy rivers, believing that they have washed away their sins and are reborn again. In countless religious creation accounts, water is seen as the source of life itself, as well as a sign of rebirth and a giver of new life. It can be a natural sign and symbol for creation, destruction, purification, rebirth, and love. Christ, as the source of "living water," walked on water and changed water into wine; thus, these acts alone can be seen as a transcendence of the natural condition represented by water or as "graced nature."[5]

Water has historically been seen to be a natural sign in the created universe of the divine presence of the Creator. In China, six hundred years before Christ was born, a poet-philosopher by the name of Lao-Tse, the author of the *Tao*, wrote these words concerning water:

> The supreme good is like water, which is the source of nourishment to almost all the living creatures on earth. It gives life to thousands of things without striving and competing. . . . It is content with the low places that people disdain. . . . One cannot reflect in streaming water. Only those who know internal peace can give it to others. . . . Have patience. Be still and allow the mud to settle and wait until the water is clear. . . . Water will wear away rock, which is rigid and cannot yield. As a rule, whatever is fluid, soft, and yielding will overcome whatever is rigid and hard. This is another paradox: what is soft is strong . . . the river and the sea are sovereign over the valleys because they take the "lower position."
>
> By being submissive and flowing wherever it can go, water is powerful. . . . All streams flow to the sea because it is lower than they are. Humility gives it its power.[6]

After reading the words of Lao-Tse in the *Tao*, it would be virtually impossible not to see water as "graced nature" or a symbol of the Creator in creation. As a natural symbol of purity, cleansing, rebirth, and renewal, the presence of water in the natural world can reveal much to us spiritually about the real presence of God. Finally, it's no coincidence that Jesus Christ, the fountain of life, called Himself "the living water."

Some Final Thoughts on Creation

First, a few thoughts from the Holy Father, the late Pope Francis, on God's presence in creation from his encyclical, *Laudato Si*

> The misuse of creation begins when we no longer recognize any higher instance than ourselves, when we see nothing else but ourselves. (13)

> In the Judeo-Christian Tradition, even the word "creation," has a broader definition and meaning than "nature." Because it has also to do with God's loving plan in which every creature has value and significance. . . . God is intimately present to each being. . . . His divine presence ensures the growth of each being and continues the work of creation. (76) (80)

> The Eucharist joins heaven and earth. It embraces and penetrates all creation. The world which came forth from God's hands returns to him in blessed and undivided adoration. In the bread of the Eucharist, creation is projected toward divinization. (236)[7]

To conclude this chapter on creation and the real presence of God, I'll summarize with this thought: The beauty, complexity, and order of the universe are testaments to God as its Creator. This should make it clear to us that the natural world, the vastness of the cosmos, and the intricacy of each individual human life are much more than merely random occurrences. They reflect the hand of a divine intelligence behind them. To think otherwise is to ignore the evidence before our eyes that points to the presence of God as its Author and Creator.

Some people believe that the created world came into existence by accident some billions of years ago as the result of a randomly massive universal explosion called the "Big Bang Theory." Consequently, many believe that there is no God who is the Creator and author of all creation. This is tantamount to believing that long ago, there was once a massive explosion at an auto assembly plant in Sussex, England, and this is how the Rolls-Royce automobile was first created and came into existence.

Notes

1   "Epiphany," *Encyclopedia Brittanica*, online, https://www.britannica.com/question /What-is-Epiphany#:~:text=Epiphany%20is%20a%20Christian%20holiday,fully %20human%20and%20fully%20divine. See also Merriam-Webster Dictionary online, https://www.merriam-webster.com/dictionary/epiphany#:~:text=%3A %20a%20usually%20sudden%20manifestation%20or,illuminating%20discovery %2C%20realization%2C%20or%20disclosure

2   Ibid., Ch. 2 f 13, (CCC #300)

3   Ibid., Ch. 1, f 5, T. Aquinas, *Summa Theologica*, "grace follows nature," Questions, 109–15

4   Ibid., Ch. 1, f 2, "The Principle of Sacramentality," pp. 9–11, 264–6, 1108–9, 1196–9.

5   "Water," *Encyclopedia Brittanica*, online, https://www.britannica.com/science/ water/additional-info

6   Lao-Tse, *The Complete Tao-Te-Ching*, online, https://taoism.net/tao-te-ching -online-translation/

7   His Holiness Pope Francis, *Laudato Si, Care for Our Common Home*, encyclical (Vatican Archives, 2015, 13, 76, 80, 236), online, https://www.vatican.va/content/ francesco/en/encyclicals/documents/papa-francesco_20150524_enciclica-laudato -si.html

8

The Family, the Neighbor, the Church Community, and Real Presence

The Family

Where there is love between persons, there is a family paradigm. God is in their midst because "God is love and whoever remains in love remains in God and God remains in them" (1 Jn 4:16). God is present in the midst of all the abundant joy and dysfunctional frustration of our family life. If a sacrament is a visible, grace-filled sign of a greater invisible reality, then the family can be seen as a sign or sacrament of the greater church community or even perhaps as that of the Holy Trinity.[1] Where there exists loving-kindness, flowing life, and receptivity among a communion of persons, God is present in their midst, whether they are conscious of His presence or not. On the other hand, just as the church community is a sacrament of the Kingdom of God, in a similar way, the family is a sacrament of the Trinity. The difference in both cases is that where human persons are involved, whether in the family or the church community, what will be missing is complete perfection. Both the Trinity and the Kingdom of God are eternally perfect realities reflecting God's real presence and mirroring it to society and the world. That being said, the human family should strive to be a model of social life, present not only to the church community but also to society at large. The members of the family, like the Trinity as a family of persons, should be present to each other and express their love for one another in word and life.

It is understood that not all families today have their basis in the Sacrament of Marriage, but the United States Conference of Catholic Bishops tells us this about the importance of marriage to the family unit:

> Marriage is a source of blessing to the couple, to their families, and to society and includes the wondrous gift of co-creating human life. Indeed, as Pope John Paul II never tired of reminding us, "the future of humanity depends on marriage and the family."

And the Catholic Catechism stresses the importance of the Sacrament of Matrimony both to God and to the future of the family and humanity:

> Marriage in God's Plan—Sacred Scripture speaks throughout of marriage and its "mystery," its institution and the meaning God has given it, its origin and its end, its various realizations throughout the history of salvation, the difficulties arising from sin and its renewal "in the Lord" in the New Covenant of Christ and the Church . . . God himself is the author of marriage. . . . Marriage is not a purely human institution despite the many variations it may have undergone through the centuries in different cultures, social structures, and spiritual attitudes. . . . The well-being of the individual person and of both human and Christian society is closely bound up with the healthy state of conjugal and family life. (CCC#1602–1603)[2]

Love within the family and the commitment to the good of the other within the family unit should flow first from the parent(s)' love of God and then each one's love and their respect for the dignity of each family member. The parent(s) should set the example by being the first and primary presence of Christ within the family. Here again, we are told in the Catholic Catechism just how much value is placed by the church community on the family and how it is considered "the domestic church":

> In our own time, in a world often alien and even hostile to faith, believing families are of primary importance as centers of living, radiant faith. For this reason, the Second Vatican Council, using an ancient expression, calls the family the "Domestic Church." It is in the bosom of the family that parents are by word and example . . . the first heralds of the faith with regard to their children. (CCC #1655)

The Christian family constitutes a specific revelation and realization of ecclesial communion, and for this reason it can and should be called a "domestic church." It is a community of faith, hope, and charity; it assumes singular importance in the Church, as is evident in the New Testament. (CCC #2204)

The Christian family is the first place of education in prayer. Based on the sacrament of marriage, the family is the "domestic church" where God's children learn to pray as the Church and to persevere in prayer. For young children in particular, daily family prayer is the first witness of the Church's living memory as awakened patiently by the Holy Spirit. (CCC#2685)[3]

God is always real and present to us in so many different ways. When we realize this, all the Bible verses concerning how to treat each other with love, care, concern, and kindness take on added importance. When we recognize Christ's presence at the center of our relationships, our marriages, families, church community, and society will gradually be transformed.

On the other hand, as we stated in an earlier chapter, we also must realize that the word "family" itself is a word constituted with meaning because the meaning of this word has changed dramatically over time. A Christian family no longer always implies that we are speaking simply of a father, a mother, and some children. Today, any single Christian parent or set of parents still has the obligation to foster love of God and love of neighbor within each member of their family unit. Additionally, each member of the Christian family unit should intend to bring to their neighbor in society and the church community, the presence of Christ, including the poorest, weakest, and most vulnerable members. Love of neighbor and life in the church community has, to a great degree, often passed first through the presence of Christ in the family.

The Neighbor

The neighbor can be seen as a surrogate for a sacramental encounter with the presence of Christ. The encounter with the presence of God can't be separated from an encounter with the neighbor. We first see the sun by looking at its rays on the mountains. Jesus Christ is often present to us as the Word of God in the Sacred Scriptures as well and thereby calls us to:

> Love God with all our heart, soul, mind, and strength and love our neighbor as our self. (Lk. 10:25–27; Mk 12:31)

Before these words were spoken by Jesus and recorded in the Gospels, they were rooted long before that in the divine revelation to the Israelite community as recorded in the Torah (see Deut. 6:5; Lev. 19:18). If we cannot love the neighbor we can see, how can we love God who is the unseen Holy Mystery? In order to experience the presence of God in our neighbor and love them, we must first ask the Holy Spirit to enlighten and empower us to see the neighbor as another "self."

The etymology of the word "neighbor" comes from an old Anglo-Saxon word, *neah*, which means "near,"[4] but with the many rapid advances in technology, transportation, and communication, the world has become a much smaller place, and everyone today is nearby to some degree. In the Christian understanding of one's neighbor, it would include our loving-kindness toward every individual because they have the grace of God's presence, and our recognition of the human dignity inherent in the entire family of the human race. "Neighbor," is then linked to the fellowship of humankind, the Father's sonship in Jesus Christ, the redemption of all humanity won by Christ's cross, and the consideration that the neighbor is one in whom the spirit of the living God is dwelling. Our love for the neighbor is no longer a command under the law, but the loving recognition and respect for every individual as an extension of the grace of God, and our personal practice of the virtue of Christian charity.

In his Papal Encyclical, *Deus Caritas Est/* "God is Love," Pope Emeritus Benedict XVI discusses how love of neighbor and love of God are so united as to be inseparable some thirty-five times throughout this relatively brief letter. Toward the end of Section One, the Holy Father tells us this:

> The First Letter of John shows us that such love is explicitly demanded. The unbreakable bond between love of God and love of neighbor is emphasized. One is so closely connected to the other that to say that we love God becomes a lie if we are closed to our neighbor or altogether hate him. Saint John's words should rather be interpreted to mean that love of neighbor is a

path that leads to the encounter with God, and that closing our eyes to our neighbor also blinds us to God.[5]

An example of the Christian attitude of love of the neighbor was first summed up by Christ in His Parable of the Good Samaritan (Lk. 10:29–37). Ultimately, we might ask the same question that was asked of Jesus in this parable, and that is "Who is my neighbor?" Given the tense relationship between Jews and Samaritans at the time of Jesus, the Parable of the Good Samaritan would have been quite shocking and surprising to its first listeners. At the time, a neighbor was thought to be a kinsman or someone who lived in our community or was part of our extended family. But a Samaritan? No way! Jesus expands the definition of "neighbor" even further by not only using someone who was considered a foreigner as an example but also by turning the question around and asking: "Who was neighbor to the man?" Today, we might have to update this parable to understand it better and call it "The Parable of the Good Immigrant" or perhaps "The Parable of the Good Muslim or Russian." Just as Jesus shot holes in His listeners' preconceived notions of "the neighborhood" back in the first century, we should also reflect on our own preconceived definitions of the word, "neighbor," and reconsider our often-unconscious characterizations of those living on the margins of society or even within our church community. In effect, we should consider whether there are certain people whose human dignity we have failed to recognize, let alone let them out of the box we put them in so that we might love them. Once we love those whom we might not even like, at some point, we might even be able to see the presence of Christ manifested in them.

The Church Community

According to the Catechism of the Catholic Church, the word "church" designates the liturgical assembly of the people of God, also the local community, and finally, the whole universal community of believers. These three meanings are seen as inseparable. Wherever and whenever the people of God gather to celebrate being members of the church and members of the

Body of Christ, they must remain as branches on the True Vine who is Christ in order to have life and bear any fruit (see CCC#752–755).[6] The *Constitution on the Sacred Liturgy*, from the Second Vatican Council, also tells us that Christ is present fourfold in the celebration of the liturgy in the church. First, in His Word, "since it is he himself who speaks when the holy scriptures are read in the Church." Christ is present in the person of the priest who offers the sacrifice of the Mass as presider. Christ is present as well in the bread and wine of the Eucharist through Transubstantiation, which will occur during the liturgy. These three manifestations of Christ's real presence will be discussed individually in subsequent chapters of this book. Finally, Christ is also present in the people who gather as they pray, sing, and worship as a unified church community. The church community is an extended Christian family, or more broadly speaking, a family of Christian families and neighbors. Some people may refer to this as the presence of Christ in the "Assembly." However, I prefer the term "Church Community" because it can specifically imply that there should be an obligation of the faithful to carry the presence of Christ in the people celebrating the liturgy within the church building out into the community. Through the power of the indwelling Holy Spirit and Christ's Eucharistic presence within the faithful, the people of God are empowered to bring the presence of Christ from the liturgy out into the broader community in society. Christ died for all. Recalling the parable whereby Christ left the ninety-nine sheep to go after the one lost sheep (see Mt. 18:12–14), we are called to be Christ's presence to many more who might be believers, whether by choice, fact, or potentiality. People in the broader community in society, who might represent the one lost sheep, need the presence of Christ just as much as those who participate often in the liturgy.

Jesus of Nazareth first made Himself "present" and manifest to others through His words and life. Today, Christ is also present in the group of people who gather to celebrate the liturgy as part of the church community. Jesus promised to be with His followers whenever they gathered in His name, but we who gather at Mass are then subsequently called to be His continuing presence in the world. Because He is Christ, our Good Shepherd, and we are His sheep, the risen Christ, our head, calls us to be the Body of Christ, His church. Christ asks each of us then to manifest His presence through the broader church which Vatican Council II called "The Church in the Modern World." So, we are called to take the Eucharistic presence of Christ in the liturgy out to the world and be the presence of Christ to one another; to those within our family, to our neighbors near and far, and out into the broader church community in society. As members of the Mystical Body of Christ, the celebration of the Eucharist should increase our love for one another and remind us of our responsibilities toward one another. As the church community, we need to deepen our understanding of the parts of Mass so that we can participate more in the liturgy, be engaged, and not be simply passive observers. This involves a deepening of what is our reciprocal presence so that it becomes a conscious presence and not just passively and robotically receiving the real presence of Jesus Christ in the Living Word and Sacrament.

Finally, we have a duty to always "read the signs of the times," and then to bring the presence of Christ to the world by taking on our role in this "Church in the Modern World." The following is an excerpt from *The Dogmatic Constitution on the Church-Document on the Laity* from Vatican II:

> The lay apostolate, however, is a participation in the salvific mission of the Church itself. Through their baptism and confirmation all are commissioned to that apostolate by the Lord Himself. Moreover, by the sacraments, especially Holy Eucharist, that charity toward God and man which is the soul of the apostolate is communicated and nourished. Now the laity are called in a special way to make the Church present and operative in those places and circumstances where only through them can it become the salt of the earth. (LG #33), (AA #3)[7]

In manifesting the presence of Christ to others in the broader church community in society, we should try to love others as Christ does and then share the Good News of Christ not only by our "windy words" but also by how we love and live our lives. This should include working against all the forces in our world that don't believe in the presence of the risen Christ and oppose the Gospel. We should also speak truth to power whenever necessary, battling all forms of prejudice, marginalization, inequality, or injustice. Finally, we should work diligently along with the hierarchy and the leadership of the institutional church to either remove or transform the many unjust systems, structures, and institutions in society. This is going to be impossible to achieve without the Holy Spirit working with and within us. Unless the Holy Spirit is working to transform our hearts and then stirring other hearts in our society and culture to be more receptive and willing to change systems, structures, and institutions, none of this will occur. We need more power than simply our own willpower. We need the same power that created the universe, which is dwelling in us within the Body of Christ.

Spirit-filled evangelizing means evangelizers must be fearlessly and joyfully open to the working of the Holy Spirit, for how can we really love our neighbor if we don't even like him? Or how can we change systems, structures, and institutions, reverse environmental blight, or change economies based on conspicuous consumption if the people responsible for these decisions remain unreceptive? Only the Holy Spirit, who is the "Spirit of Truth," can empower us to speak "truth to power," and that can only begin with opening our hearts to receive more Holy Spirit love, joy, peace, patience, kindness, generosity, faithfulness, gentleness, and self-control (Gal. 5:22). When my neighbor sees more fruit of the Holy Spirit being produced in my life, then my neighbor will believe that I "truly" love my neighbor as myself. The Holy Spirit can do it; all we have to do is open the door to our hearts to let her in. That door to our hearts, which might now be closed, will only open one way from our side with more fervent prayer and reflection. God always wants to give us the grace and the gifts of the Holy Spirit once the door is opened. Come Holy Spirit!

Notes

1   Ibid., Ch. 7 f 4, "Principle of Sacramentality."

2   Ibid., Ch. 2, f 13 (CCC # 1602–1603) see also "Marriage and Family UCCB," online: https://www.usccb.org/topics/marriage-and-family-life-ministries/marriage-and-family

3   Ibid., Ch. 2, f 13 (CCC #1655, #2603, #2685)

4   "Neighbor" from Etymology online Dictionary, https://www.etymonline.com/search?q=neighbor

5   His Holiness Pope Benedict XVI, Emeritus, *Deus Caritas Est* (Vatican Archives, 2005), online https://www.vatican.va/content/benedict-xvi/en/encyclicals/documents/hf_ben-xvi_enc_20051225_deus-caritas-est.html

6   Ibid., Ch. 2, f 13 (CCC # 752–755)

7   Ibid., Ch. 3, f 4 Vatican II Conciliar Documents, see *Dogmatic Constitution on the Church*, Lumen Gentium #33 / see also *Apostolicam Actuositatem*, Document on the Laity #3.

9

The Priest and Real Presence

Through the Sacrament of Holy Orders and by ordination, the Catholic priest, united in communion with the bishops in holy dignity, is called to be present in the person of Christ to serve God and God's people in the church. He is called to represent the presence of Christ in performing Sacramental actions as well as playing a key role in officiating at other various church celebrations. When the priest is acting *in persona Christi,* (in the person of Christ), the priest cannot act apart from Christ and the church, as all priests participate in the one priesthood of Christ, the high priest. Through the ordained ministry, the presence of Christ is made visible in the midst of the community of believers. However, the presence of Christ in the priest is not to be understood as preserving him from sin and any human failings or weaknesses, as this is the case with all human beings. On the other hand, this cannot impede the fruit of grace the priest offers the faithful in the Sacraments on behalf of Jesus Christ and the church, and which the faithful receive through the dynamic action of the Holy Spirit.[1]

Following the Council of Trent in 1545, priests of the church were given vastly improved theological and spiritual training. It wasn't until the Second Vatican Council, beginning in 1962, that there began a much greater emphasis on pastoral training and the combining of theological, spiritual, and pastoral emphasis for the seminary education of priests. This renewed emphasis, which allowed for the addition of a more pastoral education for priests, enabled them to see their priestly role in a new light as being modeled after Christ, the Good Shepherd. This way, they could be more present to the faithful of the church community as Christ was present as a shepherd to His sheep. However, as the Holy Father, the late Pope Francis, has cautioned all bishops and priests worldwide:

In order to be a good shepherd, you must also smell like the sheep.[2]

Being in the image of Christ, our forever-eternal high priest, the Catholic priest is consecrated to preach the Gospel, as the Word of God, to shepherd the faithful, build up the Body of Christ, and especially to be present to celebrate the Sacraments and preside at divine worship. Finally, in living out the mystery of love found in the Eucharist, he is to renew and apply the sacrifice of the Holy Mass as Christ's offering of Himself as the lamb of God until He comes again. The priest will do this recalling that on the night before He was to suffer and die, the Lord Jesus shared one last meal with His disciples. During this meal, our Savior shared what was to be the first Eucharistic Banquet and the soon-to-be institution of the Sacrament of the Eucharist as a sharing in His Body and Blood. He did this to perpetuate the sacrifice of the Cross throughout the ages that would follow and to entrust to the church as His spouse a living memorial of His death and resurrection. As the Gospel of Matthew tells us:

> While they were eating, Jesus took bread, said the blessing, broke it, and giving it to his disciples said, "Take and eat; this is my body." Then he took a cup, gave thanks, and gave it to them, saying, "Drink from it, all of you, for this is my blood of the covenant, which will be shed on behalf of many for the forgiveness of sins. I tell you, from now on I shall not drink this fruit of the vine until the day when I drink it with you new in the kingdom of my Father." (Mt. 26:26–29; cf. Mk 14:22–24, Lk. 22:17–20)

Recalling these sacrificial words of Christ, we profess along with the priest that, in the celebration of the Eucharist, bread and wine really become the body and blood of Jesus Christ through the power of the Holy Spirit, the instrumentality of the priest, and the eating of the bread and the drinking of the wine by the faithful. This change from bread and wine into the body and blood of Christ is called "Transubstantiation." We can speak of the Real Presence of Christ in the Eucharist because this Transubstantiation has occurred. The transforming power of this word alone is important, particularly because language can sometimes change the perspective of reality (CCC#1376).[3]

As it was thousands of years ago in the early Christian community and still is the case today at the liturgy, Christ is present in His Word, in the bread and wine being consecrated, in the gathering of the faithful there present, and in the presence of Christ in the priest. At the liturgical celebration, the sacrifice of Jesus

Christ will be re-presented on the altar by an ordained priest or bishop. During the consecration, when the priest says, "Take this, all of you and eat of it, for this is my body," Jesus Christ is speaking through him. As mentioned earlier, in Latin this is called *in persona Christi* as the priest stands "in the person of Christ," the eternal high priest. At this time, these words spoken by the priest have transforming power. Through the presence of Christ working through the words spoken by the priest, those gathered to celebrate the Real Presence of Christ in the Eucharist together are able to participate in an ongoing Sacramental encounter in the course of history. Christ's real presence saves us from our sins and opens up the possibility of spending eternal life with God. The event itself is occurring both in time and in the timelessness of eternity. The celebration of the Eucharist is taking place at a particular sacramental moment in time as the priest consecrates the bread and wine. However, at the liturgical celebration, eternity and time will be intersecting. Because our God is all-loving and "the way, the truth, and the life," we believe Him when He tells us: "I will be with you always, until the end of the age" (Mt. 28:20). By His real presence in the Eucharist, Christ is thereby fulfilling His promise to be with us always into eternity.

The Eucharist will strengthen us for the spiritual journey to eternal life. The bread and wine are veiled and will still remain bread and wine at that moment in time. The presence of Jesus Christ is Sacramental; it is real but hidden. However, the body and blood of Christ we receive through Transubstantiation at the Eucharistic Banquet do give us a foretaste of eternal life because that intimate union with the real presence of the Lord is not only taking place in time for us but in eternity as well. Eternal life is mystically occurring in that present and now-moment in time. Real Presence involves not only a change from bread and wine into Christ's body and blood but also an anticipated change in us that occurs when we "eat the bread and drink the wine" with childlike trust and openness.

In the Dogmatic Constitution on the Church, *Lumen Gentium*, which was one of the primary and foundational documents put forth at Vatican Council II, we find the following statement:

> Priests exercise their sacred function especially in the Eucharistic worship or the celebration of the Mass by which acting in the person of Christ and proclaiming his mystery they unite the prayers of the faithful with

the sacrifice of their head and renew and apply in the sacrifice of the mass until the coming of the Lord the only sacrifice of the New Testament namely that of Christ offering Himself once for all a spotless victim to the Father. (LG # 28)[4]

As Catholics, we know that symbols can be very powerful. The church uses them often during liturgical celebrations. For example, the crucifix behind the altar reminds us of the costly price paid in sacrificial love for us and forgiveness of our sins by Jesus Christ. Also, the lit Sanctuary Candle next to the tabernacle reminds us that Christ is present inside, and He is the light of the world. Symbols like these and many others in our church touch us in several ways that go beyond any mere words. With these Christian symbols in mind, is it any wonder that the Tradition of our Catholic Church has always been that the priest represents the presence of the risen Lord Jesus on the altar? The priest is also there on the altar, representing symbolically the presence of the risen Lord at each of the celebrations of the Sacraments of our church. In addition to the celebration of the Eucharist, the priest is present and celebrates along with the faithful at the Sacraments of Baptism, Confirmation, Penance, Anointing of the Sick, and Matrimony. It is through the priests of our church that Jesus Himself ministers to us His Sacramental graces because Christ Himself is the only real, true, invisible yet present minister of each Sacrament. The priest is the ordained and visible representative and instrument of Jesus Christ. He plays a vitally important role in the church, especially during the Sacrament of Penance, to give us God's gifts of forgiveness, mercy, and reconciliation. The priest in the Sacrament of Confession is acting in the person of Jesus Christ (*in persona Christi*). When the priest absolves the penitent, he doesn't say, "God absolves you from your sins," but rather "I absolve you from your sins" because he is acting in the person of Christ at that moment. On the other hand, the priest is fully aware that it is only God who can forgive our sins. The priest also challenges us to have the same kind of compassion we've received and to forgive others the way we have been forgiven. Through confession with the priest, we can repent and place ourselves in the presence of God working through the action of the priest in the power of the Holy Spirit, be absolved, and then be reconciled to Christ and the church.[5]

In summation, the presence and work of the priest are to bring God's Holy Spirit to the people and to bring the people to the Holy Spirit of God. In doing this, he prays for and with the people of God, preaches the Gospel, and teaches the message of Jesus Christ through Word and Life. He re-presents Christ as he presides and celebrates the holy sacrifice of the Mass and nourishes the people's spiritual hunger by feeding the souls of the faithful. The priest is a type of Christ, the Good Shepherd, in performing his pastoral role. He baptizes, participates with the bishop at the Sacrament of Confirmation, welcomes newcomers into the church, witnesses and celebrates marriages, visits the sick and the dying, comforts and encourages those suffering, and when and where necessary, is present to defend the souls of the faithful through his teaching and promulgating sound church doctrine.

At the end of our lives on earth, the priest will be present one last time to commit us to finally and potentially be in the presence of God and meet God face to face. Because of our belief in our immortal soul and the resurrection of our body, the priest will act with loving-kindness at our funeral rites. With solemn prayers for the faithful left behind and presiding at a public funeral rite, he will accompany our remains, along with our loved ones, to comfort and strengthen them upon our death. He will preside at our final Eucharistic celebration in this earthly life, as acting in the person of Christ; he will bury our bodily remains with care befitting the temple of God within us. Only our remains will then be buried separately, as the spiritual bond that unites us with the Holy Spirit of God will stay alive and return to the Lord who gave it.[6] As the Apostle Paul tells us in his letter to the Romans:

> For I am convinced that neither death, nor life, nor angels, nor principalities, nor present things, nor future things, nor powers, nor height, nor depth, nor any other creature will be able to separate us from the love of God in Christ Jesus our Lord. (Rom. 8:38–39)

Notes

1   Ibid., Ch. 2, f 13, (CCC # 1544–1568), online, https://www.usccb.org/sites/default/files/flipbooks/catechism/390/

2   His Holiness Pope Francis, "Shepherd must smell like the sheep," Vatican News, 2013, online, https://www.vaticannews.va/en/pope/news/2021-06/pope-francis-priests-students-church-louis-french.html

3   Ibid., Ch. 2, f 13, (CCC# 1376)

4   Ibid., Ch. 3, f 4, Vatican Council II, 1965, Pastoral Constitution on the Church (Lumen Gentium #28)

5   Ibid., Ch. 1, f 2, "Principle of Sacramentality." See also Ibid, Ch. 1 f 3, pp. 1477–87

6   Ibid., Ch. 2, f 13, USCCB, An Overview of Catholic Funeral Rites, online https://www.usccb.org/prayer-and-worship/sacraments-and-sacramentals/bereavement-and-funerals/overview-of-catholic-funeral-rites

10

The Living Word and Real Presence

Ignorance of the Scriptures is ignorance of Christ.

—St. Jerome[1]

Sacred Scripture as God's living word is filled with mystery, but no more than the real presence of God, who is the Holy Mystery who authored it. It will then be God's Holy Spirit who takes this word, first spoken long ago in ages past, then written on ink and paper, and whispers it to us as a re-presented Living Word before writing it lovingly, indelibly, and enduringly on our hearts.

In the Old Testament, most of the references to the Word of God are to the divine word of Yahweh found first in the law, then as spoken creatively or charismatically through the psalmists, priests, and prophets (see Exod. 20:1–17, 34:27–28; Ps. 33:6, 107:20; Isa. 55:11; Jer. 23:29). It was seen as the positive reception of a dynamic reality and an entity endowed with the awe-inspiring presence of God. It is also seen to be living and effective, while being charged with penetrating power. It effects what it signifies as a creative agent of God, and though it might be delayed, the word that went forth from the mouth of God never returned void without accomplishing God's will for which it was sent. The prophet Isaiah will tell us about the enduring, real, and present power in the Word of God. This phrase will be repeated in the New Testament as God's Word then becomes a "Living Word in the flesh" as contained in the Gospel of Jesus Christ:

> The grass withers, the flower wilts, but the Word of our God stands forever. (Isa. 40:8) (1 Pet. 1:22–25)

In the New Testament, following His Incarnation, Jesus Christ becomes the Living Word of God enfleshed, and because the Kingdom is in Him, the Kingdom of God dwells in our midst. Subsequent to Jesus' crucifixion, death, resurrection, and ascension, the Word of God becomes alive and manifestly present in the developing Christian church after Pentecost with the advent of the Holy Spirit sent by Jesus from the Father. In the year 400 AD, the first widespread edition of the Bible, including the New Testament, was assembled by St. Jerome. This manuscript included all forty-six books of the Old Testament and the twenty-seven books of the New Testament. The Old Testament of the Catholic Bible included seven books from the Second Canon. The book of Revelation by St. John was added in the year 419 AD. From this time forward, the entire Bible as the Sacred Scriptures was then seen by Catholics and Christians as the complete and divinely inspired Word of God.[2]

Today, when the Living Word is read and spoken by the priest, deacon, or lector, and heard by the church community during the Eucharistic celebration, Jesus Christ is present in the Holy Spirit. The presence of the Holy Spirit in the hearts of the faithful is then stirred, and grace enables us to experience the presence of Jesus Christ among us through His Living Word, which is the source and end of all love and knowledge. The Living Word then prepares our spirit for intimate communion with God, which we will then receive more completely at our participation in the Eucharistic Banquet.

The Word of God is alive, sharp, and active. The fact that it is "living" means that it has a vital power inherent within itself. Jesus likened the Word of God to seed in Mt. 13:3–23. Seed, like the Word of God, is living; it dies first, but then it brings forth more new, glorious, and abundant life. The Living Word of God rests in no way on the authority of the preacher or proclaimer, nor is it effective through them (1 Cor. 3:5–9). The Gospel becomes effective as the Living Word of God through God's power and presence (Jer. 23:29; Rom. 1:16; Heb. 4:12). The Word of God was not only spoken to man but became man in Jesus of Nazareth; it is a person, Jesus Christ. It is not a message, doctrine, idea, philosophy, or system of thought involving intellectual apprehension. It is a divine activity of God using the power of the Holy Spirit as a spiritual manifestation of Jesus' presence (1 Cor. 12:3–12).

In the first chapter and the first verse of the Gospel of John in the Bible, he tells us:

In the beginning was the Word, and the Word was with God, and the Word was God. (Jn 1:1)

"Word" is the best English translation we can render for the Greek term *Logos*, but John's intention is to convey more than what we might consider as an item used in speech or as a part of language. It has a far more "pregnant" meaning. The Word (*Logos*, Gk.), as the Son of God, that the evangelist, John, is describing, combines first God's creative and dynamic activity, present right from the beginning of time and discussed in the Old Testament book of Genesis (Gen. 1:1). He is also describing what he sees as personified, preexistent Wisdom who was God's co-creator at the beginning as detailed in the Old Testament books of Genesis, Proverbs, and Wisdom. In using the term *Logos*, Gk., John is also revealing to us that Jesus is the ultimate intelligibility of all reality. A few verses later (Jn 1:14), he will be advising us that Jesus is not only God revealing but God revealed in the flesh and that the Incarnate Word becoming flesh is the new place of God's presence among His people that once filled the tabernacle (see Exod. 25:89; 40:34). The Word should be seen as a dynamically present reality and an entity endowed with spiritual power. Following the death and resurrection of Jesus, the Word of God in the preaching and proclaiming of the Gospel in the new Christian church will become effective through God's power, which manifests the presence of God in the Word through the Holy Spirit sent by Jesus.[3]

In the first Sacrament, Baptism, we were welcomed into the church. With the sign of the cross, we were then baptized by the priest in the name of the Father who created us, the Son who saves us through His death and resurrection, and the Spirit who is then within us and fills us with new life. The Word of God is the "Sword of the Spirit" (Eph. 6:17), and it is through the Holy Spirit that Jesus Christ is made present to us as believers who are then sealed with the Holy Spirit. The presence of God as the Word of God will then continue to stay alive in the Christian church and in the temple of God, who are all those faithful who are Baptized in the Holy Spirit.

Jesus did not simply come to proclaim the Word of God and the Kingdom of God. Jesus is the Word of God, and the Kingdom is in Him. Christ commanded His Apostles to preach and teach His Gospel as the living and effective Word of

God. The common duty to do this then became the primary work and role of the body of priests and pastors within the evolution of the Catholic/Christian Church. At Vatican Council II, we learned that it is also the role of the people of God to proclaim the Word of God in word and life or word and action and to be the "Church in the Modern World." Doing this enables the Holy Spirit of Jesus Christ to manifest Christ's presence in the Body of Christ to both believers and potential believers alike in the wider world. Christ died for all.

The Gospel is and will always be the continuing story of the cross, death, and resurrection of Jesus Christ who, as the Living Word of God, is a salvific force expressive of God's power and love (*dynamis; agape*, Gk). As we grow in the spiritual life, we recognize that the priests/pastors have their special and unique role in preaching the Word of God, but the entire Church in the modern world (Vat II), as a Sacrament of the Kingdom of God, also plays a role in proclaiming the Word of God outside of the church building. This enables the Holy Spirit to show the way to salvation for humankind in the course of the history of the world. Catholic Social Teaching shows us how to do that by honoring human dignity, loving God and neighbor, serving the least among us, hungering for social and economic justice, and embracing our role as laity with a vocation within the church in the modern world. This enables us to evangelize with and through the presence of the Holy Spirit in word and life.[4]

Vatican Council II produced an outstanding "Document on Divine Revelation," titled *Dei Verbum* (Word of God). It reaffirmed the church's role as the people of God and their pastors in continuing to preach and proclaim the presence of Jesus Christ as the Living Word of God, being revealed by the Holy Spirit. In it, we find the following pronouncements given to us on the Word of God:

> Sacred Scripture is the word of God inasmuch as it is consigned to writing under the inspiration of the Holy Spirit, while sacred tradition takes the Word of God entrusted by Christ the Lord and the Holy Spirit to the Apostles, and hands it on to their successors in its full purity, so that led by the light of the Spirit of truth, they may in proclaiming it preserve this Word of God faithfully, explain it, and make it more widely known. (9)

> Inspired by God and committed once and for all to writing, they impart the Word of God Himself without change and make the voice of the Holy

Spirit resound in the words of the prophets and Apostles. Therefore, like the Christian religion itself, all the preaching of the Church must be nourished and regulated by Sacred Scripture. In the sacred books, the Father who is in heaven meets His children with great love and speaks with them; and the force and power in the Word of God is so great that it stands as the support and energy of the Church, the strength of faith for her children, the food of the soul, the pure and everlasting source of spiritual life. (21)

Sacred theology rests on the written Word of God, together with sacred tradition as its primary and perpetual foundation. By scrutinizing in the light of faith all truth stored up in the mystery of Christ, theology is most powerfully strengthened and constantly rejuvenated by that word. For the Sacred Scriptures contain the Word of God and since they are inspired, really are the Word of God. (24)

The sacred synod also earnestly and especially urges all the Christian faithful, especially Religious, to learn by frequent reading of the divine Scriptures the excellent knowledge of Jesus Christ—Just as the life of the Church is strengthened through more frequent celebration of the Eucharistic mystery; similarly we may hope for a new stimulus for the life of the Spirit from a growing reverence for the Word of God, which "lasts forever" (Isa. 40:8; see 1 Pet. 1:23–25). (25) (26)[5]

Because Jesus is the Word of God become flesh and is the full self-communication of God through the Holy Spirit, we should show a similar reverence for the Word of God in the Bible as we do for the Eucharist. During the celebration of the Sunday Mass, the Book of the Gospels is carried aloft with honor in the entrance procession and placed on the altar until the Gospel reading to show the unity of Scripture and Eucharist. This action demonstrates to us the unifying power of the one table of the Word of God, united with Christ's Eucharistic body and blood.

God's Word is eternally living and effective, but in God's ongoing work of salvation and redemption, God desires it to become alive in you and me. The light which comes to us through the Holy Spirit, manifested in the Word of God, will illuminate the path we are to follow to show us the way to the true light, who is Jesus Christ, the Morning Star and the sun which will never set. Along with the hierarchy of the church, we, as the people of God who are laypersons with a vocation in the wider world, have been given the task of evangelization to spread the Word of God in word and life. Another soul-stirring document from Vatican II is the *Decree on the Apostolate of the Laity*, which tells us:

> The laity exercise the apostolate in fact by their activity directed to the evangelization and sanctification of men and to the penetrating and perfecting of the temporal order through the spirit of the Gospel—their temporal activity openly bears witness to Christ and promotes the salvation of men. The laity, in accordance with their state of life, live in the midst of the world and its concerns; they are called by God to exercise their apostolate in the world like leaven, with the ardor of the spirit of Christ—Such a life requires a continual exercise of faith, hope, and charity. Only by the light of faith and by meditation on the Word of God can one always and everywhere recognize God in Whom "we live, and move, and have our being" (ref. Acts 17:28). (2) (4)

> The laity carry out their manifold apostolate both in the Church and in the world. In both areas there are various opportunities for apostolic activity—Since in our times women have an ever more active role in the whole life of society, it is very important that they participate more widely also in the various fields of the Church's apostolate (9)—As sharers in the role of Christ as priest, prophet, and king, the laity have their work cut out for them in the life and activity of the Church (10)—Since in our times, different forms of materialism are spread far and wide even among Catholics, the laity should not only learn doctrine more diligently, especially those main points which are the subjects of controversy, but should also exhibit the witness of an evangelical life in contrast to all forms of materialism. (31)[6]

The Holy Bible, where the Living Word of God dwells, is in a category all its own among the world's vast collection of holy books, and nothing can come close to rivaling it. Why? Because the Word, made alive and dynamically active by the Holy Spirit, can do things other words simply can't. When the Holy Spirit in the Word of God enkindles the Holy Spirit being lit in the believer, what happens then can only be described as a blazing bonfire of the Spirit. Furthermore, the Living Word, because it is also a word of truth, will tell us instinctively how to be and not to be, how to act and not to act, how to pray and not to pray. This is because the Holy Spirit in the Word is a "Spirit of truth"—being, acting, and praying—not just with us and through us, but in us. Finally, the manifestation of the Holy Spirit in the Word of God as the presence of Christ in believers of all time is also a "Spirit of love" which gives us a foretaste (Rom. 8:23) and a pledge (2 Cor. 1:22, 5:5) of our salvation that is promised. Love is all there is in the end, and if it's not perfect love, it's not the end (1 Cor. 13).

Maranatha-Come Holy Spirit![7]

Notes

1 St. Jerome, online quote, *The Catholic Exchange*, https://catholicexchange.com/ignorance-of-scripture-is-ignorance-of-christ-2/

2 "Books of the Bible," *United Conference of Catholic Bishops*, online, https://bible.usccb.org/bible

3 New American Bible, St. Joseph Edition (New York: Catholic Book Publishing Co., Gospel of John, Ch. 1, 1970), Ch. 1, §1, 1, see p. 145 of the New Testament.

4 Michael Hickey, *Catholic Social Teaching* (Lanham, MD: Hamilton Books, 2018), Sec. One, pp. 1–33.

5 Ibid., Ch. 3, f 4, Vatican Council II Documents, Dei Verbum, Word of God, 9, 21, 24, 25, 26, online, https://www.vatican.va/archive/hist_councils/ii_vatican_council/documents/vatii_const_19651118_dei-verbum_en.html

6 Ibid., Ch. 3, f 4, Vatican Council Documents, Document on the Laity, Apostolicam Actuositatem, 2, 4, 9, 10, 31 online, -https://www.vatican.va/archive/hist_councils/ii_vatican_council/documents/vat-ii_decree_19651118_apostolicam-actuositatem_en.html.

7 Ibid., Ch. 2, f 4, "Word of God" Jerome Biblical Commentary, Sec. 48, pp. 14–20, 57:41, 58:10, 61:25, 35, 62, 63:120, 64:82, 77:45, 46, 79:30, 125, see also Ch. 1, f 3, "Word of God," K. Rahner, *Encyclopedia of Theology*, pp. 1821–8.

11

The Ascension, the Eucharist, and Real Presence

In the Gospel of John, Chapter 1, we read the following about the divine origins of Jesus Christ:

> In the beginning was the Word, and the Word was with God, and the Word was God. He was in the beginning with God. . . . And the Word became flesh and made his dwelling among us. (Jn 1:1, 14)

If the exalted Lord of the universe and the preexistent master of creation could compress His Being into the tiny body of a baby to be born a human being in Mary's womb and become incarnate as Jesus of Nazareth—is it then such a leap of faith for us to believe that following His mystical absence in the crucifixion, resurrection, and Ascension, He would be really present to us in the elements of the bread and wine of the Eucharist? Every celebration of the Eucharist is a participation in the one sacrifice of Jesus Christ on Calvary. The Eucharist can be seen as what the meaning of the Ascension is all about. To talk about the Eucharist and the Ascension in one breath is paradoxical, to say the least, in that we are speaking simultaneously about the absence and the real presence of Jesus Christ. It is the context in which what is called, "Transubstantiation," is occurring and is the manner in which both the Ascension and the Eucharist are to be understood. When we receive the bread and wine, we receive the body and blood of Christ in time and space, while in the Ascension, Christ is exalted and eternally present before the Father in heaven as our advocate and intercessor. In that now-moment, time and space on earth intersects with eternity in heaven as the continuation of history intersects with Divine Providence.[1] In speaking about Transubstantiation and the bread and wine of the Eucharist becoming the body and blood of Christ St. Ambrose has said:

If the word of the Lord Jesus is so powerful as to bring into existence things which were not, then those things which already exist can be changed into something else.[2]

The Ascension of Jesus Christ can be described as the exaltation of Christ, entering into His final glory at the right hand of the Father. This had been foretold in the prophetic book of Daniel, as Daniel's prophecy spoke of a mysterious savior called "one like a son of man" ascending on a cloud. This mysterious and angelic being approaches the throne of God, where He receives divine glory, honor, and eternal kingship as Daniel writes:

As the visions during the night continued, I saw coming with the clouds of heaven One like a son of man. When he reached the Ancient of Days and was presented before him, He received dominion, splendor, and kingship; all nations, peoples and tongues will serve him. His dominion is an everlasting dominion that shall not pass away, his kingship, one that shall not be destroyed. (Dan. 7:13–14)

At its center, the Ascension signifies a transition of the risen Christ to that of the exalted Christ. It is certainly linked with His resurrection, but also with His continuing Eucharistic and Holy Spirit real presence in the church as the Body of Christ. It is also linked with His Paschal Mystery, His glorification, and His Second Coming (*Parousia*). In Christ's human nature, the humanity in which we all share has entered into the inner life of God in a new and exalted way. What this implies is that "heaven" now means that we as human persons have a place in the heart of God. This exaltation and Ascension are hidden from the eyes of much of the world. It is a veiling which is indicated in Scripture throughout the Old Testament and in the New Testament through the continual reference to a "cloud" (Exod. 24:15; Acts 1:9).

The Gospels, as well as the book of Acts, tell us that Christ's Ascension occurred forty days after His resurrection. Here is what appears in the Gospels of Mark and Luke and the book of Acts:

And so, the Lord Jesus, when he had finished speaking to them, was taken up to heaven, and is seated now at the right hand of God. (Mk 16:19)

Also:

> When he had led them out as far as Bethany, he lifted up his hands and blessed them; and even as he blessed them, he parted from them and was carried up into heaven. (Lk. 24:50–51)

And:

> The Ascension of Jesus.

> When they had gathered together they asked him, "Lord, are you at this time going to restore the kingdom to Israel?" He answered them, "It is not for you to know the times or seasons that the Father has established by his own authority. But you will receive power when the Holy Spirit comes upon you, and you will be my witnesses in Jerusalem, throughout Judea and Samaria, and to the ends of the earth." When he had said this, as they were looking on, he was lifted up, and a cloud took him from their sight. While they were looking intently at the sky as he was going, suddenly two men dressed in white garments stood beside them. They said, "Men of Galilee, why are you standing there looking at the sky? This Jesus who has been taken up from you into heaven will return in the same way as you have seen him going into heaven." (Acts 1:6–11)

The Ascension of Christ is similarly discussed in Lk. 24:51; Eph. 4: 8–10; and 1 Pet. 3:22. Also, in the Gospel of John, Jesus will prophecy as follows:

> And I, when I am lifted up from the earth, will draw all men to myself. (Jn 12:32)

Initially, this would signify Jesus being "lifted up" on the cross. Ultimately, it would announce His Ascension into heaven. Being "lifted up" in the Ascension will mark His exaltation and the definitive entrance of His humanity into God's heavenly domain, where He is seated at the right hand of God to intercede on our behalf. Furthermore, in four other chapters in the Gospel of John, Jesus had already prophesied that His Ascension was to occur after His resurrection (see Jn 1:51; 3:3, 7, 13, 31; 6:61–62; 20:17). And the factuality of its occurrence was later discussed among his followers in the Apostle Paul's Letters to the Ephesians (Eph. 4:8–10) and 1 Tim. 3:16. In the resurrection and Ascension, Jesus of Nazareth would rise and ascend to become the Universal Christ, having been given supreme authority from the Father and exalted Lordship over all of creation. Several centuries after John's Gospel was written, these Johannine verses above would be used in part to make reference to the Ascension of Jesus Christ, and to form a statement of Christian creedal belief. They would help to form what we now refer to as "The Apostle's Creed" in which we recite:

> He ascended into heaven and is seated at the right hand of God, the Father Almighty.[3]

Jesus Himself had told His disciples that He was going to go away because only then would He send them the Holy Spirit from the Father (Jn 16:7–16), and that is what happened on the Day of Pentecost, ten days after Jesus' Ascension. The Holy Spirit descended on the church with awesome power, thus inaugurating a new age in the history of the world—the age of the Holy Spirit's presence in the church as the Body of Christ. The Apostle Peter connects Jesus' resurrection, exaltation, and Ascension with the outpouring of the Holy Spirit on the people of God as follows:

> God raised this Jesus; of this we are all witnesses. Exalted at the right hand of God, he received the promise of the Holy Spirit from the Father and poured it forth, as you see and hear. (Acts 2:32–33)

The Ascension was not simply the last of Jesus' resurrection appearances; it is different. Jesus suddenly disappears while the Apostles watch. After the resurrection, Jesus appears as different but in a recognizable form. Here Jesus will say to Mary Magdalene, "Stop holding on to me, for I have not yet ascended to the Father" (See Jn 20:11–18, 21:1–14). However, after His Ascension, He will be transformed. His appearance on the Emmaus Road (Lk. 24:13–35) and Saul's experience of Jesus appearing to him on the Damascus Road are evidence of this (Acts 9:1–19). The conversion of Paul under the influence of his experience of Jesus' transformation will be even further proof, as Paul will become a divinely chosen instrument in the plan of God.

St. Augustine, an early church Father, theologian, and often referred to as "The Doctor of Grace," said this about the Ascension, and our own future bodily resurrection in one of his homilies given on the Feast of the Ascension:

Today our Lord Jesus Christ ascended into heaven; let our hearts ascend with him. Listen to the words of the Apostle: If you have risen with Christ, set your hearts on the things that are above where Christ is seated at the right hand of God; seek the things that are above, not the things that are on earth. For just as he remained with us even after his Ascension, so we too, are already in heaven with him, even though what is promised us has not yet been fulfilled in our bodies.[4]

In the Middle Ages, St. Thomas Aquinas, in his *Summa Theologica*, describes the necessity for the Ascension to have followed Christ's resurrection with these words:

The place ought to be in keeping with what is contained therein. Now by His Resurrection Christ entered upon an immortal and incorruptible life. But whereas our dwelling-place is one of generation and corruption, the heavenly place is one of incorruption. And consequently, it was not fitting that Christ should remain upon earth after the Resurrection; but it was fitting that He should ascend to heaven.

The Ascension of Christ and His real presence in the bread and wine of the Eucharist, at first glance, seem almost contradictory: Jesus is present in the Eucharist but absent because of His Ascension. Despite this conundrum, we realize that the Eucharist is not a substitute for the absence of the ascended Jesus, but more the sacramental disclosure of exactly what the Ascension means. The Ascension of Jesus will prove to be not only a disappearance but also a parting that will end only at the Second Coming of Christ at the *Parousia*. On the other hand, Jesus had already told us that He will be with us always, until the end of time, so His ascended presence should be seen more as a transformation and, moreover a "Transubstantiation" than a total absence. Anytime and anyplace the Holy Spirit in us as believers meets the Real Presence of Christ in the Eucharist, there is continuing evidence of this. Furthermore, this is also an indication that in the here and now, the so-called "present," we can enter into both Christ's present and our own future bodily resurrection, transformation, and Ascension.

Because of the mysterious nature of the Ascension, there may be a tendency on the part of some scholars and theologians to overly spiritualize it. If the resurrection is a bodily occurrence, and we are to believe in a future resurrection of the body, how could we believe that the Ascension of Jesus is strictly something spiritual and not corporeal? Aquinas argued against this in his *Summa* as follows:

> The more exalted place is due to the nobler subject, whether it be a place according to bodily contact, as regards bodies, or whether it be by way of spiritual contact, as regards spiritual substances; thus a heavenly place which is the highest of places is becomingly due to spiritual substances, since they are highest in the order of substances. But although Christ's body is beneath spiritual substances, if we weigh the conditions of its corporeal nature, nevertheless it surpasses all spiritual substances in dignity, when we call to mind its dignity of union whereby it is united personally with God. Consequently, owing to this very fittingness, a higher place is due to it above every spiritual creature. Hence Gregory says in a Homily on the Ascension (*xxix in Evang.*) that: "He who had made all things, was by His own power raised up above all things." . . . This comparison may be considered either on the part of the places; and thus there is no place so high as to exceed the dignity of a spiritual substance: in this sense the objection runs. Or it may be considered on the part of the dignity of the things to which a place is attributed: and in this way it is due to the Body of Christ to be above spiritual creatures.[5]

Furthermore, in his book *Miracles*, the Christian writer and apologist C. S. Lewis also objects to any strict spiritualization of the Ascension of Jesus Christ. He insists that after the Ascension, Christ was not exclusively a spiritual being. Here is what he writes:

> We can (spiritualize the Ascension) only if we regard the Resurrection appearances as those of a ghost or hallucination. For a phantom can just fade away; but an objective entity must go somewhere—something must happen to it. And if the Risen Body were not objective, then all of us, whether Christian or not, must invent some explanation for the disappearance of the corpse.[6]

Finally, to many of us as Christian faithful who seek the presence of Jesus Christ in our lives, the Ascension of Jesus Christ, following His resurrection, may seem like it is more a kind of separation from us than anything else because

Christ has now left us and ascended back to the Father in heaven. The words of Karl Rahner, S. J., one of the foremost theologians of our time, can shed some light on this and bring us some comfort and consolation in this regard. Here is what he writes in one of his books, *The Eternal Year*, regarding the Ascension as it follows the bodily resurrection of Christ:

> In the incarnation, the eternal Word of the Father compressed himself into our flesh . . . my faith and my consolation are centered on this, that in his Ascension, Jesus has taken with him everything that is ours. He has ascended and sits at the right hand of the Father. . . . The absolute *Logos* shall look at me in eternity with the face of a man. . . . The Ascension seems to be a separation. But it is separation only for Our paltry consciousness. We must will ourselves to believe in his nearness— in the Holy Spirit.[7]

In conclusion, Jesus Christ, in ascending, has become for us the Kingdom of Heaven. The Ascension of Jesus following His bodily resurrection is a great mystery and a profound paradox. Christ ascending and returning to the Father's side ended His post-resurrection appearances. On the one hand, this creates a source of great sorrow, for He is now absent from us. On the other hand, it is simultaneously a cause of great joy because He has never been closer and more present to us. This comes about through His Holy Spirit which He sent from the Father and is now alive in us as the Body of Christ, as well as His presence in His Living Word in the Sacred Scriptures, and in His Real Presence in our celebration of the Eucharist, which we will discuss at length in the next chapter. Our hope is in God, Father, Son, and Holy Spirit. Jesus Christ is enthroned and exalted in heaven with the Father and seemingly absent from us while remaining present with us on earth in the power of the Holy Spirit as we celebrate the Eucharistic Banquet. There is no separation in the Trinity, only unity. If there is any seeming separation, it exists only in our "paltry consciousness," as Fr. Karl Rahner has said above. As Jesus told us, He will never leave us. What He has created for us in His Ascension and the Eucharist is to transform the mystery of His absence in the Ascension into the reality of His Eucharistic real presence.

Notes

1 "Transubstantiation," Ibid., Ch. 1, f 2, pp. 826–30. Ibid., Ch. 1, f 3, pp. 1751–5.

2 St. Ambrose, "Transubstantiation," *de Sacramentis*, IV, pp. 5–16, https://oll
.libertyfund.org/titles/ambrose-on-the-mysteries-and-the-treatise-on-the
-sacraments

3 Ibid., Ch. 2, f 13, "Apostles Creed," United Conference of Catholic Bishops, The
Credo, CCC# 184, p. 49, online https://www.usccb.org/prayers/apostles-creed

4 St. Augustine, quote, Vatican Archives, From a sermon by Saint Augustine, bishop
(Sermon de Ascensione Domini, Mai 98, 1–7: PLS 2, pp. 429–95), online, https://
www.vatican.va/spirit/documents/spirit_20010525_agostino_en.html

5 Ibid., Ch. 1, f 5; Thomas Aquinas, Quotes, *Summa Theologica*, Tertia Pars, Q. 57,
online, https://www.newadvent.org/summa/4057.htm

6 C. S. Lewis, *Miracles, The Ascension* (London: HarperCollins, 1998), online,
https://www.google.com/books/edition/Miracles/tH8di3qQDhEC?hl=en&gbpv=1
&printsec=frontcover

7 "The Ascension," K. Rahner, *The Eternal Year* (Vancouver, BC: Kessinger
Publishing, 1964), pp. 1–144.

12

The Eucharistic Banquet and Real Presence

Theology of Eucharistic Real Presence

It was St. Anselm who gave us the original definition of theology as "faith seeking understanding."[1] God reveals His truth to us in ways that we can understand through the gift of faith and the grace of the Holy Spirit dwelling in us and in His church. As regards the real presence of Jesus Christ in the Eucharist, we are thus enabled to understand at least in some small measure what would otherwise remain unknown to us, though we can never completely comprehend this Transcendent Reality of God's mysterious presence. If we believe in God's real presence in the Eucharist, we can at least partially understand. As a result, our faith in the real presence of the Lord deepens and increases.

In our understanding of Catholic theological language, in the act of consecration during the celebration of the Eucharist, the "substance" of the bread and wine is changed by the power of the Holy Spirit into the "substance" of the body and blood of Jesus Christ. This occurs in the present while the appearances of bread and wine will remain. Our faith will also continue to remain in the unseen. What will continue to be seen, touched, and tasted is the bread and wine. Through the presence and power of the Holy Spirit, this in fact is now the body and blood of Christ at the level of "substance" and in the deepest reality of God's true presence. Thus, in the Eucharist, the bread ceases to be bread in substance and becomes the Body of Christ, while the wine ceases to be wine in substance and becomes the Blood of Christ. As was stated in the previous chapter, this change at the level of "substance" from bread and wine into the Body and Blood of Christ is called "Transubstantiation." According to the tenets of our Catholic faith, we can speak of the Real Presence of Christ in the Eucharist because this Transubstantiation has occurred both as a transcendental reality and as a Holy Mystery in the present moment as well as in eternity (cf. Catholic Catechism, no.1376).[2]

As was stated previously, although the body and blood of Christ in the Eucharist represent the single most unique example of the understanding of the theology of Real Presence, it is not the only one. At the Eucharist banquet, Christ is present in the person of the priest who offers the sacrifice of the Mass. Christ is present in His Word since it is He Himself who speaks when the holy scriptures are read in the church. He is also present in the assembled people of God as we pray, for He has promised:

> Where two or three are gathered together in my name there am I in the midst of them. (Mt. 18:20)

We speak of the presence of Christ under the appearances of bread and wine as "real" to underscore the special nature of that presence. In celebrating the Eucharist, this presence is called "real" not to exclude the idea that others are "real" too, but rather to indicate a special, unique, and substantial Real Presence. In the Eucharist, Christ is "real" in the fullest sense of the word, and His "presence" is unique and unsurpassable. There is more to Christ's Eucharistic Real Presence than all the other ways we have previously discussed. Finally, in our understanding of the theology of real presence, we must never attempt to limit God merely to our understanding. We should allow our understanding to be stretched by our further discovery of God's revelation as it is unveiled to us gradually by the Holy Spirit.

In light of the fact that the Eucharist has been referred to as "the Body and Blood of Christ" since the time of Jesus' Last Supper and the beginnings of the early Christian church, it is appalling to think that, according to a report from the Pew Research Center, a large number of Catholics don't believe in the Real Presence of Jesus Christ in the Eucharist. The Real Presence of Christ in the Eucharist is not meant to be taken as something symbolic, metaphorical, or figurative. Real means real.[3] Is it any more or less difficult to believe in Christ's Real Presence in the Eucharist than it is to believe in the Immaculate

Conception, the virgin birth of Christ, the resurrection, or the Holy Spirit? Probably not; it just takes faith. It was St. Bernard of Clairvaux who cautions us with the following statement: "Theology must be rooted in scripture and fed by prayer to negate the hubris of human intellect."[4]

The Living Bread

Bread is both a sign and symbol of the staff of life, and we need it to sustain our natural life here on earth. Jesus Christ, as "the Living Bread" is a Sacrament of God. The theme of bread takes up all of Chapter 6 of the Gospel of John as it moves from the "Multiplication of the Loaves" into "The Bread of Life Discourse." Although bread is both a sign and a symbol, it is closer to a symbol in John. By definition, a "symbol" is a sign that embodies what it signifies. Therefore, when Jesus says, "I Am the Living Bread," He is embodying the sign of bread. However, even the word "symbol" is close, but it is not as descriptive or relevant to what Jesus is implying here as is the word "Sacrament." A Sacrament is a visible, grace-bearing sign of an invisible reality. The reality relates to God's presence. What John, the writer of this last of the four canonical Gospels written (90 AD), is trying to show us is that the Eucharistic reality is beyond the sign and symbol of the bread. The Real Presence of Jesus, who is the Sacrament of the Living God, is in His being both the "Living Bread" and the "Bread of Life."

The Bread of Life Discourse

Our Lord Jesus Christ, on the night before He suffered the passion of the cross, shared one last Passover meal with His disciples. During this meal, our Savior initiated what was to be the Sacrament of His body and blood. In doing this, He perpetuated for all time His sacrifice of the cross and thus entrusted to the fledgling Church a memorial of His death and resurrection. In creatively adapting the Jewish Passover meal, Jesus gave an entirely new meaning to it. He was to become the paschal lamb as the Passover offering. The new "Passover" was to commemorate a new "Exodus" from sin and death for God's people in union with Him and His Eucharistic real presence of flesh and blood. Following the Last Supper, which the evangelist John also relates in Chapter 6 of his Gospel, Jesus gives us what is called "The Bread of Life Discourse." We believe these are not simply dead words in the Bible, but a living word meant for us today. Here is what He tells believers and disbelievers alike, then and now:

> I am the living bread that came down from heaven; whoever eats this bread will live forever; and the bread that I will give is my flesh for the life of the world. The Jews quarreled among themselves, saying, "How can this man give us his flesh to eat?" Jesus said to them, "Amen, amen, I say to you, unless you eat the flesh of the Son of Man and drink his blood, you do not have life within you. Whoever eats my flesh and drinks my blood has eternal life, and I will raise him on the last day. For my flesh is true food, and my blood is true drink. Whoever eats my flesh and drinks my blood remains in me and I in him." (Jn 6:51–56)

God is infinitely simple, and these are simple words. Those of us who believe in the real presence of Jesus Christ in the Sacrament of the Eucharist do not take these words of Jesus in the Gospel of John to be meant abstractly, metaphorically, symbolically, conceptually, or figuratively.

The bread and wine represent Jesus' actual giving of Himself on the cross for the life of the world. Real presence means just that—"real presence." Jesus is truly presenting Himself to us in giving us the bread and wine. The Jerome Biblical Commentary confirms that Jesus' words in response to those gathered who disbelieve do not encourage any mistaken figurative understanding of His pronouncement. Jesus is identifying the institution of the Eucharist with Himself as the son of man.[5] *Eucharistio*, is the word that is used here in the Greek language, and it means "giving thanks." It is a verb, and it implies that the bread and wine are being dynamically, spiritually, actively, and substantially changed into the body and blood of Jesus Christ and His "giving" of Himself. The verb is used to show dynamic action, and it implies it is happening in the now-moment as it is used in the present tense. Furthermore, the verb used for "eating" in these verses is not the classical Greek verb used for human eating, but that of animals "munching" or "gnawing." This may be part of John's intended emphasis on the reality of the eating of the flesh and blood of Jesus (cf. Jn 6:55). "Flesh and blood" is also the common Old Testament expression which referred to human life.

The noun *eucharist* also originates from the Greek language, and it is translated to mean, "thanksgiving."[6] It implies from that part of the word used, which is (*charis*, Gk.), that there is a "gift of loving-kindness" being presented. In the celebration of the Eucharist, Jesus is not only giving us bread and wine but His body and blood. He is gifting us Himself in the past and in the future as an eternal "present" in this now-moment. We can only praise God for the sublime gift of Jesus' eternal and unique sacrifice as we prayerfully assemble, and our church, through its priest, "re-presents" this gift while allowing us to share in the banquet with thanksgiving.

Eucharistic Adoration and Real Presence

In Eucharistic adoration, we become present to the Real Presence of the Lord. Real Presence is not something that can be "taught," as it must be "caught." We do not grasp it as much as it grasps us. Often in our prayer time, as is the case before the celebration of the Eucharist, or at our presence in Eucharistic adoration, silence before the Holy Eucharist as loving adoration is our best initial approach. This is because, first and foremost, we are in the presence of Jesus Christ who, as our Lord and God, is both a Transcendent Reality and the ultimate Holy Mystery. Eucharistic Real Presence is a profound reality and mystery that cannot be explained fully in words. Adoration itself is a human act offered to God to acknowledge both His real presence in our midst and His infinite character, supreme perfection, omniscience, and our dependence upon Him for our very created life and our forgiveness of sins. Although fundamentally different, the adoration we show to the Lord present in our midst should extend to the reverence and love we should show to any finite person created by God because they possess presence, an inherent, sacred character, and human dignity. The worship of Jesus Christ as the Son of God, and given to Him as God, is designated by the Greek name *latreia* for which the best translation in the English language is the English word "adoration."

Adoration differs from other acts of worship in that it formally consists of our self-abasement before the one true God in devout recognition of His mystical transcendence and real presence among us. Our call to express the worship of the Lord in spirit and truth by our silent adoration has been reaffirmed in the words of Christ in the Gospels:

The Lord your God you shall adore, and him only shall you serve. (Mt. 4:10)

At the Last Supper, Christ instituted the wonderful Sacrament of the Eucharist for His worshippers and adorers of all time. Here He makes Himself present to us in memory of His sacrifice on the cross and the glory of His resurrection, which became the center of all history—past, present, and future. As the Sacrament of God, Jesus instituted this sacramental mystery of the Eucharist and entrusted it to the church. Christ told us: "Do this in memory of me" (Lk. 22:19). Therefore, the Eucharist can be defined as both Jesus Christ's gift of His real presence to us and the gift of ourselves back to Him in praise, worship, and adoration. In the celebration of the Eucharist, all time and space have subsequently become filled with Christ. This implies that in the oneness of our lives in Christ, any moment in time and space can thus become a present moment of Eucharistic adoration. Because Jesus Christ is eternally present, placing ourselves in the presence of God in His Eucharist enables us to listen and allows Him to speak to us in God's language, which is Holy Silence.

This silent adoration of Jesus Christ present in the Eucharist grew out of the teaching of the Gospel writers and St. Paul. They made it plain to the Apostolic Church that the Eucharistic elements were literally and substantially Jesus Christ continuing His saving mission among us. Christ's real presence, has been confirmed by many of the early church Fathers from the first through the fifth century such as Ignatius of Antioch, Justin Martyr, Origen, Cyril of Jerusalem, and Theodore of Mopsuestia. The real presence of Jesus Christ in the Eucharist can be seen as a vital continuation of the Apostolic Tradition of our church. John, the evangelist, wrote the last of the four canonical Gospels in the year 90–95 AD. Ignatius of Antioch, one of the first church Fathers, was a living and direct disciple of John. Ignatius, as bishop of Antioch, before he died in the year 107 AD, wrote a unifying letter to the Church of Philadelphia in Asia, outlining the continuing Apostolic Tradition of the Real Presence of Jesus Christ in the Eucharist. Ignatius' words are as follows:

> Take care then to partake of the one Eucharist, for one is the flesh of our Lord, Jesus Christ and one is the cup to unite us with his blood on the one altar, just as there is one Bishop assisted by the presbyters and the deacons.[7]

The Theology of Real Presence was then confirmed in the theology of the last of the Greek Fathers, St. John Damascene, around the year 700 AD, when he made the following concrete statement:

> The bread and wine are not a foreshadowing of the body and blood of Christ—by no means! It is the actual deified body of the Lord, because the Lord Himself said: "This is my body"; not "a foreshadowing of my body" but "my body," and not "a foreshadowing of my blood" but "my blood."[8]

It was then reaffirmed once again in the Middle Ages in Question 75 of the *Summa* of St. Thomas Aquinas. Also, in the Middle Ages, the Council of Trent would declare that Christ should be worshipped and adored now in the Eucharist no less than He had been in first-century Palestine because:

> In the Eucharist, it is the same God whom the apostles adored in Galilee.[9]

Today, our One, Holy, Apostolic Church further reaffirms the Real presence of Christ in the Eucharist in many sections of the modern Catholic Catechism as well (see CCC #1322 through #1419).[10]

Jesus Christ dwells in the Eucharist today just as surely as He dwelt in the village of Nazareth long ago. In mystical communion, He makes Himself present and accessible in each heart which knows Him interiorly and desires to know Him more perfectly. In the Eucharist, God's silence is the deepest as we are alone with the Lord and can allow Him to speak to our heart center where, in loving tenderness, Deep can speak to deep—Presence to presence. Just like Peter, John, and James on the mountain at the transfiguration, we fall silent in gazing at Jesus—we are in each other's presence and "alone together."

At Vatican II in 1965, several of the Church's documents praised the adoration of the Real Presence of Christ in the Eucharist. The Council Document, "Dogmatic Constitution on the Church," (*Lumen Gentium*), extensively treats real presence, and another document, the Council's "Constitution on the Sacred Liturgy," (*Sacrosanctum Concilium*) praises those who seek to investigate more profoundly and to understand more fruitfully the doctrine of real presence in the Holy Eucharist.

> Christ is always present in His Church, especially in her liturgical celebrations. He is present in the sacrifice of the Mass, not only in the person of His minister—but especially under the Eucharistic Species. (SC no. 7)[11]

So, Eucharistic Adoration is a sign of silent devotion to and worship of Jesus Christ, who is believed by Catholics to be really present, body, blood, soul, and divinity, under the appearance of the consecrated host; that is, sacramental bread. This silent adoration is based on the tenet of the real presence of Christ in the Blessed Sacrament. Catholic doctrine holds that at the moment of consecration, the elements of bread and wine are changed (substantially) into the body, blood, soul, and divinity of Christ while the appearances (the "species") of the elements remain. In the doctrine of real presence, at the point of consecration, the act that takes place is a double miracle:

1) Christ is present in a physical form.
2) The bread and wine have truly, substantially become Jesus' body and blood.

The word, "Eucharist," can be seen as both a noun and a verb (*Eucharist*; *Eucharisteo*, Gk.). In my personal experience of encountering the Real presence of Christ in the Eucharist, I have often realized that I have that experience more completely when I've envisioned the Eucharist as a verb, in the dynamic action, and not only the object. It is true, of course, that the bread and wine really become the body and blood of Christ, but Christ is also present in the "eating of the bread" and the "drinking of the wine." Furthermore, Christ is really present in His "gifting" and our "receiving" of His body and blood. During Eucharistic adoration, Christ is present, but also manifests in His "transforming" as well as in our "adoring." It is a matter of our experiencing real presence both in adoring through the Eucharistic action (verb) as well as the object of the Eucharist (noun).

In his book, *The Power of Silence*, Robert Cardinal Sarah has this to say about silence, love, adoration, and presence:

Humanity advances toward love through adoration. Sacred silence, laden with the adored presence, opens the way to mystical silence, full of loving intimacy.[12]

Hopefully, what any of us might take away from our time spent in Eucharistic adoration is an experience of the real presence of Christ in loving silence. This experience oftentimes manifests itself to the world as our attempts to demonstrably express our love of God and neighbor. For any of us, our adoring needs to move out from the time we spend experiencing God's presence in Eucharistic adoration in the church building to experiencing and adoring God's presence in our family and our neighbors in the wider world around us. God is everywhere, in everyone and everything, and always present. What does it mean to be silently praying before the Lord, present in the Eucharist as the Bread of Life? Our hunger for material food in some ways can be compared to the hunger in our heart and soul for the Lord. We can use the occasion of Eucharistic adoration to truly reflect on what it means to: "Work for the food that endures to eternal life" (Jn 6:27).

Silent adoration can make the next time that we are able to receive the Eucharist at Mass as both physical and spiritual food all the more meaningful. We humans will always hunger. Jesus shows us that our hunger is not just for any material food, but for God. When He feeds us with the bread and wine of the Eucharist, He feeds our bodies with His body and nourishes our souls with His divinity. In encouraging us to come into the Lord's presence in Eucharistic adoration, the Holy Father, the late Pope Francis, has told us:

> Immersing oneself in silent Eucharistic adoration is the secret to knowing the Lord. . . . One cannot know the Lord without being in the habit of adoring, of adoring in silence. . . . To waste time—if I may say it—before the Lord—before the mystery of Jesus Christ. To adore, there in the silence, in the silence of adoration. He is the Lord, and I adore Him.[13]

Our silence before the Lord can induce adoration as a form not only of worship but also of deep love, awe, and reverence. Since friends who love each other visit regularly and come into each other's presence, any visit to the Blessed Sacrament for the practice of silent adoration is sometimes referred to as "the practice of loving Jesus Christ." As we kneel or sit in silent adoration before this piece of bread, Christians can gaze at the face of God present. In some ways, this can be compared to spouses who might gaze into each other's faces in loving adoration. Their real presence to each other needs no words and is a silent spiritual and loving embrace. After a time, the practice of Eucharistic adoration might even allow us to not only gaze into the face of God present but also to see the face of God in the face of our spouse, the face of a friend, a child, a neighbor—or perhaps even a complete stranger.

Eucharistic adoration is not simply a private alternative of what ought to be a deeply communal celebration; rather, it ought to lead those who encounter it back to the heart of that communal Eucharistic mystery where we celebrate together the Christ who is *Emmanuel*, that is, "God with us." Therefore, before the presence of Jesus Christ in the Eucharist, I must continue to attempt to recognize my sinfulness, empty myself of all pride and self-seeking ambition, beg God's forgiveness, and allow myself to be filled with the joy of being in His real presence while I am also being present to the Lord.

At the end of this book, as I look back and reflect on what I've written, my only regret is that I wish I could have simplified the Theology of Real Presence more than I have. Perhaps you will try to understand that discussing transcendent realities such as real presence, Transubstantiation, adoration, sacramentality, "in persona Christi," and Ascension, and so on, is not so simple to put into words. As was stated earlier in this book, this is especially the case because they are grounded in faith experiences and lend themselves much more to being "caught" than "taught." They grasp us before we can grasp them. Faith becomes such an important factor in understanding these transcendent realities. You might recall that the definition of theology is "faith seeking understanding." To speak about these transcendent realities in words implies that the Holy Spirit needs to reveal the words we use, but first needs to hold our hand as we take baby steps and walk little by little with the Lord present at our side to guide us.

Therefore, I will leave you with a simple but true story of someone whose words and wisdom reveal a far deeper understanding of what "Real Presence" truly means. There is an ancient story about St. John Vianney who in church one day came upon a very old peasant farmer who was simply staring at the

Eucharistic tabernacle. Upon asking the farmer what he was doing, the farmer replied:

Nothing, I look at Him and He looks back at me.[14]

I believe that the old farmer knew more than most of us about the Real Presence of Jesus Christ.

Notes

1 St Anselm, "Theology," *Encyclopedia of Philosophy*, online, https://plato.stanford .edu/entries/anselm/#FaiSeeUndChaPurAnsThePro

2 Ibid., Ch. 2, f 13, UCCB, United Conference of Catholic Bishops, (CCC# 1376)

3 Ibid., Ch. 2, f 4, Jerome Biblical Commentary, Sec. 42:86, 43:184, 48:153–155, 45:24, 51:71, 61:66, 62:26, 63:24, 93–97, 71:87

4 Bernard of Clairvaux, *Catholic Insight*, online, https://catholicinsight.com/ appreciating-the-wisdom-of-the-last-of-the-fathers-saint-bernard-of-clairvaux/

5 Ibid., Ch. 2, f 4, Jerome Biblical Commentary, see Sec. 42:86, 43:184, 48:153–155, 45:24, 51:71, 61:66, 62:26, 63:24, 93–97, 71:87

6 "Eucharisto," (Gk.), online, https://www.biblestudytools.com/lexicons/greek/kjv/ eucharistos.html#:~:text=Eucharistos%20Definition,others%2C%20winning%2C %20liberal%2C%20beneficent

7 Ibid., Ch. 1, f 5, Ignatius of Antioch, Epistle to the Philadelphians, New Advent Church Fathers, online, https://www.newadvent.org/fathers/0108.htm

8 St. John Damascene, "*The Orthodox Faith*, IV [PG 94, 1148–49])."

9 Ibid., Ch. 1, f 5, Aquinas, T., Summa Theologica, Q. 75, New Advent online, https://www.newadvent.org/summa/4075.htm

10 Ibid., Ch. 2, f 13, UCCB, United Conference of Catholic Bishops, (see CCC #1322 through #1419), online https://www.catholiccrossreference.online/catechism/#!/ search/1322-1419.

11 Ibid., Ch. 3, f 4, Vatican II Council Documents, Dogmatic Constitution on the Church, (Lumen Gentium), Constitution on the Sacred Liturgy, Sacrosanctum Concilium (SC #7), Vatican Archives online, https://www.vatican.va/archive/hist _councils/ii_vatican_council/documents/vat-ii_const_19631204_sacrosanctum -concilium_en.html

12 Cardinal Robert Sarah, *The Power of Silence*, quote, (San Francisco, CA., Ignatius Press, 2017) see also online https://prodigalcatholic.com/2017/05/10/top-10 -favourite-quotes-from-cardinal-sarahs-book-the-power-of-silence/

13 His Holiness Pope Francis, Aleteia, *Adoration of the Eucharist*, quote online, https://aleteia.org/2016/10/20/pope-francis-eucharistic-adoration-is-the-secret -to-knowing-the-love-of-jesus-christ

14 Ibid., Ch. 2, f 13, "St. John Vianney," UCCB, United Conference of Catholic Bishops, CCC# 2715, quote online, https://www.catholicculture.org/culture/ library/catechism/index.cfm?recnum=6996

About the Author

Michael Hickey is a graduate of Northeastern University, Boston, MA, and a Master of Divinity Studies graduate of Weston Jesuit/Boston College School of Theology and Ministry, Boston, MA. Following a career as a corporate executive for a Fortune 500 company, he became a director of two 501 C-3 charitable nonprofits.

He has had eight books previously published: *Get Wisdom, Get Goodness, Get Real, Get to the End, Catholic Social Teaching, Themes from The Gospel Of John, Holy Silence,* and *Rising Light.* The last seven books were published by University Press of America and Hamilton Books/Rowman & Littlefield Publishing Co., Lanham, MD.

Mr. Hickey is retired and spends spring and summer with his family in Dartmouth, MA, and fall and winter in Naples, FL. He teaches courses on Religion and Philosophy at Florida Gulf Coast University, RA, Naples, FL, and occasionally facilitates Zoom Bible study classes.

His current work, *Real Presence,* is based on material he will be using in teaching a new course at FGCU.

Michael Hickey is married to Theresa, a published poet and the initial editor of all his books. In their almost sixty years of marriage, they have raised four happy and "well adjusted" children into adulthood, and they have seven grandchildren.

Index

www.ingramcontent.com/pod-product-compliance
Lightning Source LLC
Chambersburg PA
CBHW060545100426

42742CB00013B/2458

9780761880714